# Two Tragedies

Medea and The daughters of Troy

Ella Isabel Harris

**Alpha Editions**

This edition published in 2020

ISBN : 9789354042546

Design and Setting By
**Alpha Editions**
www.alphaedis.com
email - alphaedis@gmail.com

# Two Tragedies of Seneca

## Medea and The Daughters of Troy

Rendered into English Verse, with an Introduction

By

## Ella Isabel Harris

The Riverside Press

Boston and New York
Houghton, Mifflin and Company
The Riverside Press, Cambridge
M DCCC XCIX

# CONTENTS

# INTRODUCTION

# I

THE interest of English students in the dramas of Seneca lies in the powerful influence exerted by them upon the evolution of the English drama, and these translations have been undertaken in the hope that they may be found useful to English students of English drama.

Though all the tragedies ascribed to Seneca are not by the same hand, yet they are so far homogeneous that in considering them as a literary influence, one is not inclined to quarrel with the classification that unites them under a single name. For the present purpose, therefore, no time need be spent in the discussion of their authorship or exact date, but we may turn at once to look for their appearance as agents in the development of the modern, serious drama. In this relation it is hardly possible to overestimate their determining influence throughout Europe. Perhaps it may have been owing to the closer racial bond between the Romans and the French that while the Senecan influence upon the drama in France was so overmastering and tyrannical, in England the native spirit was stronger to resist it, and the English drama at its best remained distinctively English, the influence exercised over it by the Senecan tragedies being rather formative than dominant.

Before the time of Marlowe and Shakespeare the forces that determined the development of the serious drama in England were practically twofold : one native, emanating from the moralities and miracle plays ; the other classic, and found in the tragedies long ascribed to Seneca. These remnants of the Roman drama were known to the English at a very early date, were valued by the learned as the embodiment of what was best in ancient art and thought, and were studied in the Latin originals by pupils in the schools even while the schools were still wholly monastic. During the latter half of the sixteenth century, separate plays of Seneca were translated into English by various authors, and in 1581 Thomas Newton collected these translations into one volume, under the title of " Seneca his Ten Tragedies, Translated into English." After an examination of these translations one can readily understand why Elizabeth felt the need of an English translation of the Latin favorite, and herself essayed to turn them into English verse. In 1702 Sir Edward Sherburne published translations of three of the plays, but the edition of 1581 still remains the only complete English translation. From the edition of 1581 I quote a part

of the translation of the beautiful lines on the
future life, Troades, Act II., Scene iv.: —

> " May this be true, or doth the Fable fayne,
>     When corps is deade the Sprite to live as yet?
> When Death our eies with heavy hand doth strain,
>     And fatall day our leames of light hath shet,
> And in the Tombe our ashes once be sat,
>     Hath not the soule likewyse his funerall,
> But stil (alas) do wretches live in thrall?

> " Or els doth all at once togeather die?
>     And may no part his fatal howre delay,
> But with the breath the Soule from hence doth flie?
>     And eke the Cloudes to vanish quite awaye,
> As danky shade fleeth from the poale by day?
>     And may no iote escape from desteny,
> When once the brand hath burned the body?"

In Sherburne's translation of 1702 the same
lines are rendered as follows : —

> "Is it a Truth? or Fiction blinds
>     Our fearful Minds?
> That when to Earth we Bodies give,
>     Souls yet do live?
> That when the Wife hath clos'd with Cries
>     The Husband's Eyes,
> When the last fatal Day of Light,
>     Hath spoil'd our Sight
> And when to Dust and Ashes turn'd
>     Our Bones are urn'd ;
> Souls stand yet in nead at all
>     Of Funeral,
> But that a longer Life with Pain
>     They still retain?
> Or dye we quite? Nor ought we have
>     Survives the Grave?
> When like to Smoake immixed with skies,
>     The Spirit flies,
> And Funeral Tapers are apply'd
>     To th' naked Side,
> Whatere Sol rising does disclose
>     Or setting shows," etc.

It is also interesting to compare Sherburne's version with the earlier one in the famous passage which closes the chorus at the end of the second act of the Medea; Newton's edition gives the lines as follows : —

> " Now seas controulde doe suffer passage free,
>     The Argo proude erected by the hand
> Of Pallas first, doth not complayne that shee,
>     Conveyde hath back, the kynges unto theyr land.
> Eche whirry boate now scuddes about the deepe
>     All stynts and warres are taken cleane away,
> The Cities frame new walles themselves to keepe,
>     The open worlde lettes nought rest where it lay;
> The Hoyes of Ind Arexis lukewarme leake,
>     The Persians stout in Rhene and Albis streame
> Doth bath their Barkes, time shall in fine outbreake
>     When Ocean wave shall open every Realme,
> The Wandering World at Will shall open lye,
>     And Typhis will some newe founde Land survay
> Some travelers shall the Countreys farre escrye,
>     Beyonde small Thule, knowen furthest at this day."

## As given by Sherburne these lines are : —

> " The passive Main
> Now yields, and does all Laws sustain,
> Nor the fam'd Argo, by the hand
> Of Pallas built, by Heroes mann'd,
> Does now alone complain she 's forc'd
> To Sea ; each petty Boat 's now cours'd
> About the Deep ; no Boundure stands,
> New Walls by Towns in foreign Lands
> Are rais'd ; the pervious World in 'ts old
> Place, leaves nothing.  Indians the cold
> Araxis drink, Albis, and Rhine the Persians.
> Th' Age shall come, in fine
> Of many years, wherein the Main
> M' unloose the universal Chain ;
> And mighty Tracts of Land be shown,
> To Search of Elder Days unknown,
> New Worlds by some new Typhys found,
> Nor Thule be Earth's farthest Bound."

That the influence of Seneca's plays upon the English stage came very directly may be seen from the facts known concerning their long popularity, and the consideration in which they were held as literature, whether in the original or in translation. But their influence was exerted not only by direct means ; the revival of learning in Europe brought with it a general revival of the Latin influence, and England in borrowing from Italy and France borrowed indirectly from Rome. Among the English translations made in the time of Elizabeth from French and Italian authors, we find the names of dramas modelled closely after Seneca, and intended in their English dress for presentation on the English stage ; thus indirectly also was Senecan style and thought perpetuated in the English drama.

## II

### TENDENCIES OF SENECAN INFLUENCE AS FELT BY ENGLISH DRAMA

It would hardly be possible to find a stronger contrast than that between these Senecan tragedies and the early English drama as it existed in moralities and miracle plays before the classic influence made itself felt. With perhaps the single exception of "The Sacrifice of Isaac," which in its touching simplicity is truly dramatic, the moralities and miracle plays are little more than vivid narrative in which events of equal magnitude follow one another in epic profusion; the classic unities of time and place are unknown, and, so far as unity of action is observed, it is epic unity rather than dramatic. The characters are little more than puppets that pass across the stage, moved by no single inward spring of action, but determined in their movements by outward forces or temporary emotions.

In contradistinction to this epic profusion of inchoate external action, we find the authors of the Senecan tragedies choosing for their material only the closing portion of the myth which is the basis of their drama, and centring the little action they admit around the crisis of a soul's life, the real subject of their drama being some spiritual conflict. This introspectiveness, this interest in spiritual problems and soul processes, we find in the English drama only after it has come under the Senecan influence, and it is found in its most exaggerated form in those dramas which are most closely modelled after the Senecan pattern. While the first effect of this influence was to lessen the dramatic interest, it is only as the interest in the spiritual life is added to the wealth of external action that the English drama finds any true principle of dramatic unity. How far the stirrings of the Reformation aided in the development of this interest in soul problems is a question that the student of dramatic literature cannot ignore, but which is outside the present inquiry.

The consciousness of the importance to dramatic art of an inner spiritual theme as a central formative principle led to the nicer differentiation of character, — to the evolution of true dramatic personages from the puppets of the earlier drama, through a deeper inquiry into the inward springs of action.

The centralizing of the visible presentation around a spiritual theme brought about several secondary changes in English drama. The narrowing of the field of action necessitated the description of past and passing actions, which, though not admitted on the stage, were necessary to the understanding of the drama ; this led to the introduction of the stock character of messenger and of the long descriptive monologues so familiar in the classic drama. The widening of the interest in the spiritual conflict necessitated the objectifying of that conflict, and led to the introduction of the stock character of confidant, also well known to the Greek and Roman drama, and to the further introduction of long and passionate soliloquy.

This influence exercised by the Senecan tragedies on the material of the English drama had its counterpart in an influence on the outward form, — an influence no less dominant and abiding. The tragedies of Seneca are divided, without regard to their true organic structure, into five acts ; these acts are separated by choruses, that bear much the same relation to the acts they separate as does the orchestral interlude of to-day — that is, no real relation ; such hard-and-fast division into five parts by choruses unconnected with the action is unknown to the Greek drama. The acts are again divided into scenes, this sub-division being dependent on the exits and entrances of the *dramatis personæ*, every exit and entrance necessitating a new scene.

The early imitators of Seneca copied their model closely in the arrangement of acts and scenes, and with them, as with Seneca, chorus and act division are wholly unconnected with the action of the drama ; " Gorboduc," " Tancred and Gismunda," and " The Misfortunes of Arthur," are the earliest and most faithful English copies of the Latin model. In the Shakespearian drama the adherence to this classic form is less rigid, and the playwright adds or omits the choruses at will : in " Henry Fifth," the chorus not only separates the acts, as in Seneca, but also speaks the prologue ; in " Pericles," where Gower speaks the prologue and act interludes, there is also added a lyrical monologue by the same speaker at the opening of the fourth scene of Act IV. ; while in " The Winter's Tale " the use of a chorus has dwindled to a single monologue spoken by Time at the opening of Act IV.

In the later development of the five-act division the chorus falls away, and the act division becomes not formal but organic, and coincides with the structural divisions of introduction, rising action, climax, falling action, and catastrophe; this has now become the rule for the form of the modern serious drama.

Besides the centralization of the external action around an inner spiritual theme and the fixing of the structural form, other less fundamental results of the Senecan influence are evident in the sixteenth and seventeenth century English drama. The Senecan tragedies belong to the age of the Julian successors of Tiberius, — an age when reason had lost its control, when changes were wrought by intrigue, cunning, and brute force; when vicissitudes of fortune and enormities of conduct were witnessed with the same curiosity which is excited by a fascinating drama, and with something of the same apathy, even when the spectator himself was concerned in the exhibition. The effect of this upon the Senecan tragedy was to expand the limits of what the dramatic proprieties permitted to be represented on the stage, to give in place of dramatic action brilliant and lurid rhetoric only, and to replace a true philosophy by a stoic fatalism.

The tragic and lurid realism of action and description which especially differentiate Seneca from the Greeks found its way into England by a double stream; that is, not only directly from his dramas, but also through the channel of contemporary Italian tragedy, a tragedy which Klein in his " Geschichte des Dramas " describes as a horrible caricature of the Senecan tragedy, where the pity and fear of the Greeks are turned to shuddering horror and crocodile tears. The result is seen in the riot of bloodshed and lust of the so-called tragedy of blood. What Mr. J. A. Symonds says of Marlowe's "Tamberlane" is true of this entire school : "Blood flows in rivers, shrieks, and groans, and curses mingle with heaven-defying menaces and ranting vaunts. The action is one tissue of violence and horror." Even Shakespeare reflects this influence, and in "Hamlet," "Lear," and "Macbeth," we still find this bloody and sensational tendency, though it is purified of its worst extravagances.

We have spoken of the two characters of messenger and confidant which modern drama owes to the nobler Senecan influence ; it is to the less admirable influence of his sensational realism that we owe the introduction of supernatural agencies, — of witches, ghosts, and apparitions ; these are often little more than stage machinery : in Shakespeare, however, we find them transmuted into powerful adjuncts to the dramatic effect ; compare the ghost of Tybalt, that appears to Juliet when she takes the sleeping potion, with that of Medea's brother, that appears to Medea in the last act of the Senecan tragedy of that name ; note, too, the use of the ghost in "Macbeth," in "Julius Cæsar," and in "Hamlet."

The stoic fatalism which runs like a dark thread through these tragedies of blood is, in the English as in the Senecan tragedy, the natural concomitant of all this sensational horror, and is evident in the texture of the dramas and the character of the personages, and in original as well as in quoted passages.

## III

### DIRECT BORROWINGS FROM SENECAN TRAGEDIES

WE need give but little space to remarks upon the extent to which English dramatists borrowed directly from the Roman tragedies, for such borrowings were of far less moment in the evolution of the modern drama than the more fundamental imitation of form and structure already noted; their chief interest indeed lies outside the scope of dramatic study, and is to be found in the fact that they serve to mark English sympathy for certain phases of Roman thought.

The adornment of new tragedies by portions borrowed from Seneca calls into use most frequently the phrases which are the expression of a dark and hopeless philosophy. The fatalism referred to in preceding lines as characterizing the Elizabethan tragedies of blood had a strong hold upon the English mind from a much earlier date. One need not wonder that the thought which colored so early a poem as Beowulf, and which came to the surface in the conscious philosophy of a later time to reënter literature in the works of Alexander Pope, should have attracted the

attention of Englishmen of the sixteenth century
when they found it in a writer of such literary
prestige and philosophic renown as Seneca.

A careful reader of Seneca will recognize the
borrowings of English dramatists the more readily
as such borrowings follow closely not only the
thought but the language of the original.

Mr. John W. Cunliffe, in his monograph on
" The Influence of Seneca on English Tragedy,"
has given a careful and detailed comparison with
their originals of Senecan passages in " The Misfortunes of Arthur." In a less detailed way he
indicates the borrowings of other English authors;
on pages 25, 26 of his book we find : —

" Seneca had written in the ' Agamemnon,'

' Per scelera semper sceleribus tutum est iter.'

This is translated by Studley : —

' The safest path to mischiefe is by mischiefe open
still.'

Thomas Hughes has it, in ' The Misfortunes of
Arthur,' I. 4 : —

' The safest passage is from bad to worse.'

Marston, in ' The Malcontent,' V. 2 : —

' Black deed only through black deed safely flies.'

Shakespeare, in ' Macbeth,' III. 2 : —

' Things bad begun make strong themselves by ill.'

Jonson, in ' Catiline,' I. 2 : —

> 'The ills that I have done cannot be safe
> But by attempting greater.'

Webster, in ' The White Devil,' II. 1 : —

> ' Small mischiefs are by greater made secure.'

Lastly, in Massinger's ' Duke of Milan,' II. 1, Francisca says : —

> ' All my plots
> Turn back upon myself, but I am in,
> And must go on ; and since I have put off
> From the shore of innocence, guilt be now my pilot!
> Revenge first wrought me ; murder 's his twin brother :
> One deadly sin then help me cure another.' ' '

On page 78 he quotes the following also from " Richard Third," IV. 2 : —

> " Uncertain way of gain ! But I am in
> So far in blood that sin will pluck on sin."

The student will surmise that phrases of Seneca can be traced through much of English tragedy, and that a careful reader is likely to have little difficulty in bringing together passages inspired by the Roman tragedies.

A full comparative study of the structural form of the Senecan and of the early English regular drama will be found in Rudolf Fischer's " Kunstentwicklung der Englische Tragödie." Symonds in his " Shakespeare's Predecessors," and Klein in his " Geschichte des Dramas," also touch on the debt of the modern drama to the Roman tragedies.

In the translations that follow, I have endeavored without doing violence to English idioms to give a strictly literal translation of the Latin originals, using as my text the edition of F. Leo. I wish to express my indebtedness to Prof. Albert S. Cook, and to Drs. Elisabeth Woodbridge and M. Anstice Harris, for criticism of the translation, not only with reference to its fidelity to the original, but also with regard to its English dress.

# MEDEA

# MEDEA

## ACT I

### Scene I

*Medea* [*alone*].   Ye gods of marriage;
Lucina, guardian of the genial bed;
Pallas, who taught the tamer of the seas
To steer the Argo; stormy ocean's lord;
Titan, dividing bright day to the world;          5
And thou three-formed Hecate, who dost shed
Thy conscious splendor on the hidden rites!
Ye by whom Jason plighted me his troth;
And ye Medea rather should invoke:
Chaos of night eternal; realm opposed          10
To the celestial powers; abandoned souls;
Queen of the dusky realm; Persephone
By better faith betrayed; you I invoke,
But with no happy voice.   Approach, approach,
Avenging goddesses with snaky hair,          15
Holding in blood-stained hands your sulphurous
        torch!
Come now as horrible as when of yore
Ye stood beside my marriage-bed; bring death
To the new bride, and to the royal seed,
And Creon; worse for Jason I would ask —          20

3

Life! Let him roam in fear through unknown
    lands,
An exile, hated, poor, without a home;
A guest now too well known, let him, in vain,
Seek alien doors, and long for me, his wife!
And, yet a last revenge, let him beget      25
Sons like their father, daughters like their mother!
'Tis done; revenge is even now brought forth —
I have borne sons to Jason.    I complain
Vainly, and cry aloud with useless words,
Why do I not attack mine enemies?      30
I will strike down the torches from their hands,
The light from heaven.    Does the sun see this,
The author of our race, and still give light?
And, sitting in his chariot, does he still
Run through the accustomed spaces of the sky,   35
Nor turn again to seek his rising place,
And measure back the day?    Give me the reins;
Father, let me in thy paternal car
Be borne aloft the winds, and let me curb
With glowing bridle those thy fiery steeds!      40
Burn Corinth; let the parted seas be joined!
This still remains — for me to carry up
The marriage torches to the bridal room,
And, after sacrificial prayers, to slay
The victims on their altars.    Seek, my soul —   45
If thou still livest, or if aught endures
Of ancient vigor — seek to find revenge
Through thine own bowels; throw off woman's
     fears,
Intrench thyself in snowy Caucasus.

All impious deeds Phasis or Pontus saw,          50
Corinth shall see. Evils unknown and wild,
Hideous, frightful both to earth and heaven,
Disturb my soul, — wounds, and the scattered
          corpse,
And murder. I remember gentle deeds,
A maid did these; let heavier anguish come,     55
Since sterner crimes befit me now, a wife!
Gird thee with wrath, prepare thine utmost rage,
That fame of thy divorce may spread as far
As of thy marriage! Make no long delay.
How dost thou leave thy husband? As thou
          cam'st.                                 60
Homes crime built up, by crime must be dissolved.

## Scene II

*Enter Chorus of Corinthian women, singing the marriage
song of Jason and Creusa.*

*Chorus.* Be present at the royal marriage feast,
Ye gods who sway the scepter of the deep,
And ye who hold dominion in the heavens;
With the glad people come, ye smiling gods!     65
First to the scepter-bearing thunderers
The white-backed bull shall stoop his lofty head;
The snowy heifer, knowing not the yoke,
Is due to fair Lucina; and to her
Who stays the bloody hand of Mars, and gives    70
To warring nations peace, who in her horn
Holds plenty, sacrifice a victim wild.

Thou who at lawful bridals dost preside,
Scattering darkness with thy happy hands,
Come hither with slow step, dizzy with wine,     75
Binding thy temples with a rosy crown.
Thou star that bringest in the day and night,
Slow-rising on the lover, ardently
For thy clear shining maids and matrons long.
In comeliness the virgin bride excels     80
The Athenian women, and the strong-limbed
          maids
Of Sparta's unwalled town, who on the top
Of high Taÿgetus try youthful sports;
Or those who in the clear Aonian stream,
Or in Alpheus' sacred waters bathe.     85
The child of the wild thunder, he who tames
And fits the yoke to tigers, is less fair
Than the Ausonian prince.   The glorious god
Who moves the tripod, Dian's brother mild;
The skillful boxer Pollux; Castor, too,     90
Must yield the palm to Jason.   O ye gods
Who dwell in heaven, ever may the bride
Surpass all women, he excel all men!
Before her beauty in the women's choir
The beauty of the other maids grows dim;     95
So with the sunrise pales the light of stars,
So when the moon with brightness not her
          own
Fills out her crescent horns, the Pleiads fade.
Her cheeks blush like white cloth 'neath Tyrian
          dyes,
Or as the shepherd sees the light of stars     100

Grow rosy with the dawn.   O happy one,
Accustomed once to clasp unwillingly
A wife unloved and reckless, snatched away
From that dread Colchian marriage, take thy
          bride,
The Æolian virgin — 'tis her father's will.     105
Bright offspring of the thyrsus-bearing god,
The time has come to light the torch of pine ;
With fingers dripping wine put out the fires,
Sound the gay music of the marriage song,
Let the crowd pass their jests ; 'tis only she     110
Who flies her home to wed a stranger guest,
Need steal away into the silent dark.

↳ not so silent

# ACT II

## Scene I

*Medea, Nurse.*

*Medea.*  Alas, the wedding chorus strikes my
    ears ;
Now let me die !  I could not hitherto
Believe — can hardly yet believe such wrong.  115
And this is Jason's deed?  Of father, home,
And kingdom reft, can he desert me now,
Alone and in a foreign land?  Can he
Despise my worth who saw the flames and seas
By my art conquered? thinks, perchance, all
    crime  120
Exhausted !  Tossed by every wave of doubt,
I am distracted, seeking some revenge.
Had he a brother's love — he has a bride ;
Through her be thrust the steel !  Is this enough?
If Grecian or barbarian cities know  125
Crime that this hand knows not, that crime be
    done !
Thy sins return to mind exhorting thee :
The far-famed treasure of a kingdom lost ;
Thy little comrade, wicked maid, destroyed,
Torn limb from limb and scattered on the sea  130
An offering to his father ; Pelias old
Killed in the boiling cauldron.  I have shed

8

Blood often basely, but alas! alas!
'Twas not in wrath, unhappy love did all!
Had Jason any choice, by foreign law     135
And foreign power constrained? He could have
     bared
His breast to feel the sword. O bitter grief,
Speak milder, milder words. Let Jason live;
Mine as he was, if this be possible,
But, if not mine, still let him live secure,     140
To spare me still the memory of my gift!
The fault is Creon's; he abuses power.
To annul our marriage, sever strongest ties,
And tear the children from their mother's breast;
Let Creon pay the penalty he owes.     145
I'll heap his home in ashes, the dark flame
Shall reach Malea's dreaded cape, where ships
Find passage only after long delay.
   *Nurse.* Be silent, I implore thee, hide thy pain
Deep in thy bosom. He who quietly     150
Bears grievous wounds, with patience, and a
     mind
Unshaken, may find healing. Hidden wrath
Finds strength, when open hatred loses hope
Of vengeance.
   *Medea.* Light is grief that hides itself,
And can take counsel. Great wrongs lie not
     hid.     155
I am resolved on action.
   *Nurse.*           Foster-child,
Restrain thy fury; hardly art thou safe
Though silent.

*Medea.*          Fortune tramples on the meek,
But fears the brave.
   *Nurse.*          This is no place to show
That thou hast courage.
   *Medea.*          It can never be          160
That courage should be out of place.
   *Nurse.*                    To thee,
In thy misfortune, hope points out no way.
   *Medea.*   The man who cannot hope despairs
     of naught.
   *Nurse.*   Colchis is far away, thy husband lost;
Of all thy riches nothing now remains.          165
   *Medea.*   Medea now remains!   Here's land
     and sea,
Fire and sword, god and the thunderbolt.
   *Nurse.*   The king is to be feared.
   *Medea.*                    I claim a king
For father.
   *Nurse.*   Hast thou then no fear of arms?
   *Medea.*   I, who saw warriors spring from earth?
   *Nurse.*                    Thou'lt die!   170
   *Medea.*   I wish it.
   *Nurse.*          Flee!
   *Medea.*                    Nay, I repent of flight.
   *Nurse.*   Thou art a mother.
   *Medea.*                    And thou seest by whom.
   *Nurse.*   Wilt thou not fly?
   *Medea.*                    I fly, but first revenge.
   *Nurse.*   Vengeance may follow thee.
   *Medea.*                    I may, perchance,
Find means to hinder it.

*[handwritten note:]* circular nature
an eye for an eye,
yet then do you owe another eye?

*Nurse.*          Restrain thyself     175
And cease to threaten madly; it is well
That thou adjust thyself to fortune's change.
  *Medea.* My riches, not my spirit, fortune
    takes.
The hinge creaks, — who is this?   Creon himself,
Swelling with Grecian pride.               180


## SCENE II

*Creon with Attendants, Medea.*

  *Creon.* What, is Medea of the hated race
Of Colchian Æëtes, not yet gone?
Still she is plotting evil; well I know
Her guile, and well I know her cruel hand.
Whom does she spare, or whom let rest secure?   185
Verily I had thought to cut her off
With the swift sword, but Jason's prayers availed
To spare her life.   She may go forth unharmed
If she will set our city free from fear.
Threatening and fierce, she seeks to speak with
    us;                                        190
Attendants, keep her off, bid her be still,
And let her learn at last, a king's commands
Must be obeyed.   Go, haste, and take her hence.
  *Medea.* What fault is punished by my banish-
    ment?
  *Creon.* A woman, innocent, may ask, 'What
    fault?'                                     195
  *Medea.* If thou wilt judge, examine.

*Creon.*                              Kings command.
Just or unjust, a king must be obeyed.
  *Medea.*  An unjust kingdom never long en-
    dures.
  *Creon.*  Go hence!  Seek Colchis!
  *Medea.*                              Willingly I go;
Let him who brought me hither take me hence. 200
  *Creon.*  Thy words come late, my edict has
    gone forth.
  *Medea.*  The man who judges, one side still
    unheard,
Were hardly a just judge, though he judge justly.
  *Creon.*  Pelias for listening to thee died, but
    speak,
I may find time to hear so good a plea.          205
  *Medea.*  How hard it is to calm a wrathful
    soul,
How he who takes the scepter in proud hands
Deems his own will sufficient, I have learned;
Have learned it in my father's royal house.
For though the sport of fortune, suppliant,     210
Banished, alone, forsaken, on all sides
Distressed, my father was a noble king.
I am descended from the glorious sun.
What lands the Phasis in its winding course
Bathes, or the Euxine touches where the sea     215
Is freshened by the water from the swamps,
Or where armed maiden cohorts try their skill
Beside Thermodon, all these lands are held
Within my father's kingdom, where I dwelt
Noble and happy and with princely power.        220

*(handwritten margin note):* How does gender play a role? Is she taking on a role of a man? Is it meant to be uncomfortable in that way?

He whom kings seek, sought then to wed with me.
Swift, fickle fortune cast me headlong forth,
And gave me exile.   Put thy trust in thrones —
Such trust as thou mayst put in what light chance
Flings here and there at will!   Kings have one
            power,                                          225
A matchless honor time can never take:
To help the wretched, and to him who asks
To give a safe retreat.   This I have brought
From Colchis, this at least I still can claim:
I saved the flower of Grecian chivalry,            230
Achaian chiefs, the offspring of the gods;
It is to me they owe their Orpheus
Whose singing melted rocks and drew the trees;
Castor and Pollux are my twofold gift;
Boreas' sons, and Lynceus whose sharp eye      235
Could pierce beyond the Euxine, are my gift,
And all the Argonauts.   Of one alone,
The chief of chiefs, I do not speak; for him
Thou owest me naught; those have I saved for
            thee,
This one is mine.   Rehearse, now, all my crime; 240
Accuse me; I confess; this is my fault —
I saved the Argo!   Had I heard the voice
Of maiden modesty or filial love,
Greece and her leaders had regretted it,
And he, thy son-in-law, had fallen first            245
A victim to the fire-belching bull.
Let fortune trample on me as she will,
My hand has succored princes, I am glad!
Assign the recompense for these my deeds,

Condemn me if thou wilt, but tell the fault.    250
Creon, I own my guilt — guilt known to thee
When first, a suppliant, I touched thy knees,
And asked with outstretched hands protecting
     aid.
Again I ask a refuge, some poor spot
For misery to hide in; grant a place         255
Withdrawn, a safe asylum in thy realm,
If I must leave the city.
     *Creon.*   I am no prince who rules with cruel
     sway,
Or tramples on the wretched with proud foot.
Have I not shown this true by choosing him   260
To be my son-in-law who is a man
Exiled, without resource, in fear of foes?
One whom Acastus, king of Thessaly,
Seeks to destroy, that so he may avenge
A father weak with age, bowed down with years, 265
Whose limbs were torn asunder? That foul
     crime
His wicked sisters impiously dared
Tempted by thee; if thou wouldst say the deed
Was Jason's, he can prove his innocence;
No guiltless blood has stained him, and his
     hands                •   270
Touched not the sword, are yet unstained by
     thee.
Foul instigator of all evil deeds,
With woman's wantonness in daring aught,
And man's courageous heart — and void of
     shame,

Go, purge our kingdom ; take thy deadly herbs, 275
Free us from fear ; dwelling in other lands
Afar, invoke the gods.
    *Medea.*          Thou bidst me go ?
Give back the ship and comrade of my flight.
Why bid me go alone ?   Not so I came.
If thou fear war, both should go forth, nor choice 280
Be made between two equally at fault :
That old man fell for Jason's sake ; impute
To Jason flight, rapine, a brother slain,
And a deserted father ; not all mine
The crimes to which a husband tempted me ; 285
'Tis true I sinned, but never for myself.
    *Creon.*   Thou shouldst begone, why waste the
        time with words ?
    *Medea.*   I go, but going make one last request :
Let not a mother's guilt drag down her sons.
    *Creon.*   Go, as a father I will succor them, 290
And with a father's care.
    *Medea.*         By future hopes,
By the king's happy marriage, by the strength
Of thrones, which fickle fortune sometimes shakes,
I pray thee grant the exile some delay
That she, perchance about to die, may press 295
A last kiss on her children's lips.
    *Creon.*         Thou seekst
Time to commit new crime.
    *Medea.*        In so brief time
What crime were possible ?
    *Creon.*      No time too short
For him who would do ill.

*[Handwritten margin notes: "is she at fault then truly?"; "— mother / father roles."; "caught her!"; "← feels like a lesson / moral"]*

*Medea.*                    Dost thou deny
To misery short space for tears?
    *Creon.*                    Deep dread 300
Warns me against thy prayer; yet I will grant
One day in which thou mayst prepare for flight.
    *Medea.*   Too great the favor!  Of the time
        allowed,
Something withdraw.   I would depart in haste.
    *Creon.*   Before the coming day is ushered in 305
By Phœbus, leave the city or thou diest.
The bridal calls me, and I go to pay
My vows to Hymen.


## Scene III


    *Chorus.*   He rashly ventured who was first to
        make
In his frail boat a pathway through the deep; 310
Who saw his native land behind him fade
In distance blue; who to the raging winds
Trusted his life, his slender keel between
The paths of life and death.   Our fathers dwelt
In an unspotted age, and on the shore           315
Where each was born he lived in quietness,
Grew old upon his father's farm content;
With little rich, he knew no other wealth
Than his own land afforded.   None knew yet
The changing constellations, nor could use      320
As guides the stars that paint the ether; none
Had learned to shun the rainy Hyades,

The Goat, or Northern Wain, that follows slow
By old Boötes driven ; none had yet
To Boreas or Zephyr given names.    325
Rash Tiphys was the first to tempt the deep
With spreading canvas ; for the winds to write
New laws ; to furl the sail ; or spread it wide
When sailors longed to fly before the gale,
And the red topsail fluttered in the breeze.   330
The world so wisely severed by the seas
The pine of Thessaly united, bade
The distant waters bring us unknown fears.
The cursed leader paid hard penalty
When the two cliffs, the gateway of the sea,   335
Moved as though smitten by the thunderbolt,
And the imprisoned waters smote the stars.
Bold Tiphys paled, and from his trembling hand
Let fall the rudder ; Orpheus' music died,
His lyre untouched ; the Argo lost her voice.   340
When, belted by her girdle of wild dogs,
The maid of the Sicilian straits gives voice
From all her mouths, who fears not at her bark ?
Who does not tremble at the witching song
With which the Sirens calm the Ausonian sea ?   345
The Thracian Orpheus' lyre had almost forced
Those hinderers of ships to follow him !
What was the journey's prize ?  The golden fleece,
Medea, fiercer than the raging sea, —
Worthy reward for those first mariners !   350
The sea forgets its former wrath ; submits
To the new laws ; and not alone the ship
Minerva builded, manned by sons of kings,

Finds rowers; other ships may sail the deep.
Old metes are moved, new city walls spring up 355
On distant soil, and nothing now remains
As it has been. The cold Araxes' stream
The Indian drinks; the Persian quaffs the Rhine;
And the times come with the slow-rolling years
When ocean shall strike off the chains from
   earth,       360
And a great world be opened. Tiphys then,
Another Tiphys, shall win other lands,
And Thule cease to be earth's utmost bound.

# ACT III

## Scene I

*Medea, Nurse.*

*Nurse.* Stay, foster-child, why fly so swiftly
    hence?
Restrain thy wrath! curb thy impetuous haste! 365
As a Bacchante, frantic with the god
And filled with rage divine, uncertain walks
The top of snowy Pindus or the peak
Of Nyssa, so Medea wildly goes
Hither and thither; on her cheek the stain    370
Of bitter tears, her visage flushed, her breast
Shaken by sobs. She cries aloud, her eyes
Are drowned in scalding tears; again she laughs;
All passions surge within her soul; she stays
Her steps, she threatens, makes complaint, weeps,
    groans.    375
Where will she fling the burden of her soul?
Where wreak her vengeance? where will break
    this wave
Of fury? Passion overflows! she plans
No easy crime, no ordinary deed.
She conquers self; I recognize old signs    380
Of raging; something terrible she plans,
Some deed inhuman, devilish, and wild.
Ye gods, avert the horrors I foresee!

19

Where else is anger to go?

*Medea.*　　Dost thou seek how to show thy hate,
　　poor wretch?
Imitate love!　And must I then endure　　385
Without revenge the royal marriage-torch?
Shall this day prove unfruitful, sought and gained
Only by earnest effort?　While the earth
Hangs free within the heavens; while the vault
Of heaven sweeps round the earth with change-
　　　less change;　　　　　　　　　　　　390
While the sands lie unnumbered; while the
　　day
Follows the sun, the night brings up the stars;
Arcturus never wet in ocean's wave
Rolls round the pole; while rivers seaward flow,
My hate shall never cease to seek revenge.　395
Did ever fierceness of a ravening beast;
Or Scylla or Charybdis sucking down
The waters of the wild Ausonian
And the Sicilian seas; or Ætna fierce,
That holds imprisoned great Enceladus　　400
Breathing forth flame, so glow as I with threats?
Not the swift rivers, nor the force of flame
By storm-wind fanned, can imitate my wrath.
I will o'erthrow and bring to naught the world!
Does Jason fear the king?　Thessalian war?　405
True love fears nothing.　He was forced to
　　yield,
Unwillingly he gave his hand.　But still
He might have sought his wife for one farewell.
This too he feared to do.　He might have gained
From Creon some delay of banishment.　　410

One day is granted for my two sons' sake!
I do not make complaint of too short time,
It is enough for much; this day shall see
What none shall ever hide.   I will attack
The very gods, and shake the universe!            415
  *Nurse.*   Lady, thy spirit so disturbed by ills
Restrain, and let thy storm-tossed soul find rest.
  *Medea.*   Rest I can never find until I see
All dragged with me to ruin; all shall fall            *// misery loves company*
When I do; — so to share one's woe is joy.            420
  *Nurse.*   Think what thou hast to fear if thou
            persist;
No one can safely fight with princely power.


## SCENE II

*The Nurse withdraws; enter Jason.*

  *Jason.*   The lot is ever hard; bitter is fate,
Equally bitter if it slay or spare;
God gives us remedies worse than our ills.            425
Would I keep faith with her I deem my wife
I must expect to die; would I shun death
I must forswear myself.   Not fear of death
Has conquered honor, love has cast out fear
In that the father's death involves the sons.            430
O holy Justice, if thou dwell in heaven,
I call on thee to witness that the sons
Vanquish their father!   Say the mother's love
Is fierce and spurns the yoke, she still will deem
Her children of more worth than marriage joys.            435

*Is this not a good thing?
In the name of loving her
children does she act? Is there
a lack of a male leader?*

My mind is fixed, I go to her with prayers.
She starts at sight of me, her look grows wild,
Hatred she shows and grief.
    *Medea.*                    Jason, I flee!
I flee, it is not new to change my home,
The cause of banishment alone is new;                    440
I have been exiled hitherto for thee.
I go, as thou compellst me, from thy home,
But whither shall I go? Shall I, perhaps,
Seek Phasis, Colchis, and my father's realm
Whose soil is watered by a brother's blood?    445
What land dost thou command me seek? what
        sea?
The Euxine's jaws through which I led that band
Of noble princes when I followed thee,
Adulterer, through the Symplegades?
Little Iolchos? Tempe? Thessaly?                    450
Whatever way I opened up for thee
I closed against myself. Where shall I go?
Thou drivest into exile, but hast given
No place of banishment. I will go hence.
The king, Creusa's father, bids me go,                    455
And I will do his bidding. Heap on me
Most dreadful punishment, it is my due.
With cruel penalties let royal wrath
Pursue thy mistress, load my hands with chains,
And in a dungeon of eternal night                    460
Imprison me — 'tis less than I deserve!
Ungrateful one, recall the fiery bull;
The earth-born soldiers, who at my command
Slew one another; and the golden fleece

Of Phrixus' ram, whose watchful guardian,          465
The sleepless dragon, at my bidding slept;
The brother slain; the many, many crimes
In one crime gathered.   Think how, led by me,
By me deceived, that old man's daughters dared
To slay their aged father, dead for aye!          470
By thy hearth's safety, by thy children's weal,
By the slain dragon, by these blood-stained hands
I never spared from doing aught for thee,
By thy past fears, and by the sea and sky
Witnesses of our marriage, pity me!          475
O happy one, give me some recompense!
Of all the ravished gold the Scythians brought
From far, as far as India's burning plains,
Wealth our wide palace hardly could contain,
So that we hung our groves with gold, I took          480
Nothing.   My brother only bore I thence,
And him for thee I sacrificed.   I left
My country, father, brother, maiden shame:
This was my marriage portion; give her own
To her who goes an exile.          485
    *Jason.*   When angry Creon thought to have
      thee slain,
Urged by my prayers, he gave thee banishment.
    *Medea.*   I looked for a reward; the gift I see
Is exile.
    *Jason.*   While thou mayst fly, fly in haste!
The wrath of kings is ever hard to bear.          490
    *Medea.*   Thou giv'st me such advice because
      thou lov'st
Creusa, wouldst divorce a hated wife!

*Jason.*   And does Medea taunt me with my
    loves?
*Medea.*   More — treacheries and murders.
*Jason.*                       Canst thou charge
Such sins to me?
*Medea.*            All I have ever done.        495
*Jason.*   It only needs that I should share the
    guilt
Of these thy crimes!
*Medea.*            Thine are they, thine alone;
He is the criminal who reaps the fruit.
Though all should brand thy wife with infamy,
Thou shouldst defend and call her innocent:   500
She who has sinned for thee, toward thee is
    pure.
*Jason.*   To me my life is an unwelcome gift
Of which I am ashamed.
*Medea.*            Who is ashamed
To owe his life to me can lay it down.
*Jason.*   For thy sons' sake control thy fiery
    heart.                                      505
*Medea.*   I will have none of them, I cast them
    off,
Abjure them; shall Creusa to my sons
Give brothers?
*Jason.*        To an exile's wretched sons
A mighty queen will give them.
*Medea.*                       Never come
That evil day that mingles a great race         510
With race unworthy, — Phœbus' glorious sons
With sons of Sisyphus.

*Jason.*                    What, cruel one,
Wouldst thou drag both to banishment?   Away!
*Medea.*   Creon has heard my prayer.
*Jason.*                         What can I do?
*Medea.*   For me?   Some crime perhaps.
*Jason.*                    A prince's wrath   515
Is here and there.
   *Medea.*          Medea's wrath more fierce!
Let us essay our power, the victor's prize
Be Jason.
   *Jason.*   Passion-weary, I depart;
Fear thou to trust a fate too often tried.
   *Medea.*   Fortune has ever served me faithfully.   520
*Jason.*   Acastus comes.
   *Medea.*               Creon's a nearer foe,
But both shall fall.   Medea does not ask
That thou shouldst arm thyself against the king,
Or soil thy hands with murder of thy kin;
Fly with me innocent.
   *Jason.*               Who will oppose   525
If double war ensue, and the two kings
Join forces?
   *Medea.*      Add to them the Colchian troops
And King Æëtes, Scythian hosts and Greeks,
Medea conquers them!
   *Jason.*               I greatly fear
A scepter's power.
   *Medea.*          Do not covet it.   530
   *Jason.*   We must cut short our converse, lest
      it breed
Suspicion.

*Medea.*    Now from high Olympus send
Thy thunder, Jupiter; stretch forth thy hand,
Prepare thy lightning, from the riven clouds
Make the world tremble, nor with careful hand 535
Spare him or me; whichever of us dies
Dies guilty; thy avenging thunderbolt
Cannot mistake the victim.
    *Jason.*                    Try to speak
More sanely; calm thyself.    If aught can aid
Thy flight from Creon's house, thou needst but
        ask.                                        540
    *Medea.*  My soul is strong enough, and wont
        to scorn
The wealth of kings; this boon alone I crave,
To take my children with me when I go;
Into their bosoms I would shed my tears,
New sons are thine.
    *Jason.*    Would I might grant thy prayer; 545
Paternal love forbids me, Creon's self
Could not compel me to it.    They alone
Lighten the sorrow of a grief-parched soul.
For them I live, I sooner would resign
Breath, members, light.
    *Medea* [*aside*].  'Tis well!  He loves his sons, 550
This, then, the place where he may feel a wound!
[*To Jason.*]    Before I go, thou wilt, at least, permit
That I should give my sons a last farewell,
A last embrace?    But one thing more I ask:
If in my grief I've poured forth threatening
        words,                                        555
Retain them not in mind; let memory hold

Only my softer speech, my words of wrath
Obliterate.

   *Jason.*    I have erased them all
From my remembrance.   I would counsel thee
Be calm, act gently ; calmness quiets pain.          560

                           [*Exit Jason.*

### SCENE III

*Medea, Nurse.*

  *Medea.*   He's gone!   And can it be he leaves
    me so,
Forgetting me and all my guilt?   Forgot?
Nay, never shall Medea be forgot!
Up!   Act!   Call all thy power to aid thee now ;
This fruit of crime is thine, to shun no crime! 565
Deceit is useless, so they fear my guile.
Strike where they do not dream thou canst be
    feared.
Medea, haste, be bold to undertake
The possible — yea, that which is not so !
Thou, faithful nurse, companion of my griefs   570
And varying fortunes, aid my wretched plans.
I have a robe, gift of the heavenly powers,
An ornament of a king's palace, given
By Phœbus to my father as a pledge
Of sonship ; and a necklace of wrought gold ; 575
And a bright diadem, inlaid with gems,
With which they used to bind my hair.   These
    gifts,
Endued with poison by my magic arts,

My sons shall carry for me to the bride.
Pay vows to Hecate, bring the sacrifice,        580
Set up the altars.   Let the mounting flame
Envelop all the house.


## Scene IV

*Chorus.*   Fear not the power of flame, nor
         swelling gale,
Nor hurtling dart, nor cloudy wain that brings
The winter storms; fear not when Danube
         sweeps                                       585
Unchecked between its widely severed shores,
Nor when the Rhone hastes seaward, and the
         sun
Has broken up the snow upon the hills,
         And Hermes flows in rivers.
A wife deserted, loving while she hates,        590
Fear greatly; blindly burns her anger's flame,
For kings she cares not, will not bear the curb.
Ye gods, we ask your grace divine for him
Who safely crossed the seas; the ocean's lord
Is angry for his conquered kingdom's sake;     595
         Spare Jason, we entreat!
Th' impetuous youth who dared to drive the car
Of Phœbus, keeping not the wonted course,
Died in the furious fires himself had lit.
Few are the evils of the well-known way;       600
Seek the old paths your fathers safely trod,
The sacred federations of the world
         Keep still inviolate.

The men who dipped the oars of that brave ship;
Who plundered of their shade the sacred groves
Of Pelion; passed between the unstable cliffs;
Endured so many hardships on the deep;
And cast their anchor on a savage coast,
Passing again with ravished foreign gold,
Atoned with fearful death upon the sea          610
          For violated law.
The angry deep demanded punishment:
Tiphys to an unskillful pilot left
The rudder.   On a foreign coast he fell,
Far from his father's kingdom, and he lies      615
With nameless shades, under a lowly tomb.
Becalmed in her still harbor Aulis held
The impatient ships, remembering in wrath
          The king that she lost thence.
The fair Camena's son, who touched his lyre     620
So sweetly that the floods stood still, the winds
Were silent, and the birds forgot to sing,
And forests followed him, on Thracian fields
Lies dead, his head borne down by Hebrus' stream.
He touched again the Styx and Tartarus,         625
          But not again returns.
Alcides overthrew the north wind's sons;
He slew that son of Neptune who could take
Unnumbered forms; but after he had made
Peace between land and sea, and opened wide     630
The realm of Dis, lying on Œta's top
He gave his body to the cruel fire,
Destroyed by his wife's gift — the fatal robe
          Poisoned with Centaur's blood.

Ankæus fell a victim to the boar                         635
Of Caledonia ; Meleager slew
His   mother's   brother,   stained   his   hands   with
      blood
Of his own mother.   They have merited
Their lot, but what the crime that he atoned
By death whom Hercules long sought in vain — 640
The tender Hylas drawn beneath safe waves ?
Go now, brave soldiers, boldly plow the main,
            But fear the gentle streams.
Idmon the serpents buried in the sands
Of Libya, though he knew the future well.      645
Mopsus, to others true, false to himself,
Fell far from Thebes ; and he who tried to burn
The crafty Greeks fell headlong to the deep :
            Such death was meet for crime.
Oileus, smitten by the thunderbolt,                      650
Died on the ocean ; and Pheræus' wife
Fell for her husband, so averting fate ;
He who commanded that the golden spoil
Be carried to the ships had traveled far,
But, plunged in seething cauldron, Pelias died 655
In narrow limits.   'Tis enough, ye gods ;
      Ye have avenged the sea !

# ACT IV

## SCENE I

*Nurse.* I shrink with horror! Ruin threatens
     us!
How terribly her wrath inflames itself!
Her former force awakes, thus I have seen          660
Medea raging and attacking god,
Compelling heaven.   Greater crime than then
She now prepares, for as with frantic step
She sought the sanctuary of her crimes,
She poured forth all her threats; and what before 665
She feared she now brings forth; lets loose a host
Of poisonous evils, arts mysterious;
With sad left hand outstretched invokes all ills
That Libyan sands with their fierce heat create,
Or frost-bound Taurus with perpetual snow          670
Encompasses.   Drawn by her magic spell
The serpent drags his heavy length along,
Darts his forked tongue, and seeks his destined
     prey.
Hearing her incantation, he draws back
And knots his swelling body coiling it. —          675
'They are but feeble poisons earth brings forth,
And harmless darts,' she says, 'heaven's ills I
     seek.
Now is the time for deeper sorcery.

31

The dragon like a torrent shall descend,
Whose mighty folds the Great and Lesser Bear 680
Know well; Ophiuchus shall loose his grasp
And poison flow. Be present at my call,
Python, who dared to fight twin deities.
The Hydra slain by Hercules shall come
Healed of his wound. Thou watchful Colchian
    one, 685
Be present with the rest — thou, who first slept
Lulled by my incantations.' When the brood
Of serpents has been called she blends the juice
Of poisonous herbs; all Eryx' pathless heights
Bear, or the open top of Caucasus 690
Wet with Prometheus' blood, where winter reigns;
All that the rich Arabians use to tip
Their poisoned shafts, or the light Parthians,
Or warlike Medes; all the brave Suabians cull
In the Hyrcanian forests in the north; 695
All poisons that the earth brings forth in spring
When birds are nesting; or when winter cold
Has torn away the beauty of the groves
And bound the world in icy manacles.
Whatever herb gives flower the cause of death, 700
Or juice of twisted root, her hands have culled.
These on Thessalian Athos grew, and those
On mighty Pindus; on Pangæus' height
She cut the tender herbs with bloody scythe.
These Tigris nurtured with its current deep, 705
The Danube those; Hydaspes rich in gems
Flowing with current warm through levels dry,
Bætis that gives its name to neighboring lands

And meets the western ocean languidly,
Have nurtured these.   Those have been cut at
    dawn;                                                          710
These other herbs at dead of night were reaped;
And these were gathered with the enchanted hook.
Death-dealing plants she chooses, wrings the blood
Of serpents, and she takes ill-omened birds,
The sad owl's heart, the quivering entrails cut 715
From the horned owl living; — sorts all these.
In some the eager force of flame is found,
In some the bitter cold of sluggish ice;
To these she adds the venom of her words
As greatly to be feared.   She stamps her feet; 720
She sings, and the world trembles at her song.


## Scene II

*Medea, before the altar of Hecate.*

*Medea.*   Here I invoke you, silent company,
Infernal gods, blind Chaos, sunless home
Of shadowy Dis, and squalid caves of Death
Bound by the banks of Tartarus.   Lost souls, 725
For this new bridal leave your wonted toil.
Stand still, thou whirling wheel, Ixion touch
Again firm ground; come, Tantalus, and drink
Unchecked the wave of the Pirenian fount.
Let heavier punishment on Creon wait: —            730
Thou stone of Sisyphus, worn smooth, roll back;
And ye Danaïdes who strive in vain
To fill your leaking jars, I need your aid.

Come at my invocation, star of night,
Endued with form most horrible, nor threat    735
With single face, thou three-formed deity !
To thee, according to my country's use,
With hair unfilleted and naked feet
I've trod the sacred groves ; called forth the rain
From cloudless skies ; have driven back the sea ; 740
And forced the ocean to withdraw its waves.
Earth sees heaven's laws confused, the sun and
      stars
Shining together, and the two Bears wet
In the forbidden ocean.   I have changed
The circle of the seasons : —at my word      745
Earth flourishes with summer ; Ceres sees
A winter harvest ; Phasis' rushing stream
Flows to its source ; the Danube that divides
Into so many mouths restrains its flood
Of waters — hardly moving past its shores.    750
The winds are silent ; but the waters speak,
The wild seas roar ; the home of ancient groves
Loses its leafy shade ; the day withdraws
At my command ; the sun stands still in heaven.
My incantations move the Hyades.      755
It is thy hour, Diana !
For thee my bloody hands have wrought this
      crown
Nine times by serpents girt ; those knotted
      snakes
Rebellious Typhon bore, who made revolt
Against Jove's kingdom ; Nessus gave this blood 760
When dying ; Œta's funeral pyre provides

These ashes which have drunk the poisoned blood
Of dying Hercules ; and here thou seest
Althea's vengeful brand.   The harpies left
These feathers in the pathless den they made   765
A refuge when they fled from Zete's wrath ;
And these were dropped by the Stymphalian birds
That felt the wound of arrows dipped in blood
Of the Lernæan Hydra.
The altars find a voice, the tripod moves   770
Stirred by the favoring goddess.   Her swift car
I see approach — not the full-orbed that rolls
All night through heaven ; but as, with darkened
          light,
Troubled by the Thessalians she comes,
So her sad face upon my altars sheds   775
A murky light.   Terrify with new dread
The men of earth !   Costly Corinthian brass
Sounds in thy honor, Hecate, and on ground
Made red with blood I pay these solemn rites
To thee ; for thee have stolen from the tomb   780
This torch that gives its baleful funeral light ;
To thee with bowed head I have made my prayer ;
And in accordance with my country's use,
My loose hair filleted, have plucked for thee
This branch that grows beside the Stygian wave ;   785
Like a wild Mænad, laying bare my breast,
With sacred knife I cut for thee my arm ;
My blood is on the altars !   Hand, learn well
To strike thy dearest !   See, my blood flows forth !
Daughter of Perseus, have I asked too oft   790
Thine aid ?   Recall no more my former prayers.

To-day as always I invoke thine aid
For Jason's sake alone! Endue this robe
With such a baleful power that the bride
May feel at its first touch consuming fire          795
Of serpent's poison in her inmost veins;
Let fire lurk hid in the bright gold, the fire
Prometheus gave and taught men how to store —
He now atones his daring theft from heaven
With tortured vitals. Mulciber has given          800
This flame, and I in sulphur nurtured it;
I brought a spark from the destroying fire
Of Phaeton; I have the flame breathed forth
By the Chimæra, and the fire I snatched
From Colchis' savage bull; and mixed with these 805
Medusa's venom. I have bade all serve
My secret sorcery; now, Hecate, add
The sting of poison, aid the seeds of flame
Hid in my gift; let them deceive the sight
But burn the touch; let the heat penetrate          810
Her very heart and veins, stiffen her limbs,
Consume her bones in smoke. Her burning hair
Shall glow more brightly than the nuptial torch!
My vows are paid, and Hecate thrice has barked,
And shaken fire from her funeral torch.          815
'Tis finished! Call my sons. My precious
          gifts,
Ye shall be borne by them to the new bride.
Go, go, my sons, a hapless mother's sons!
Placate with gifts and prayers your father's wife!
But come again with speed, that I may know 820
A last embrace!

fire as a metaphor for rage
↳ aims to have her fire then spread and
consume her victims. Anger spreads to
others perhaps?

## Scene III

*Chorus.*   Where hastes the blood-stained Mæ-
    nad, headlong driven
By angry love?  What mischief plots her rage?
With wrath her face grows rigid ; her proud
    head
She fiercely shakes ; threatens the king in wrath. 825
Who would believe her exiled from the realm ?
Her cheeks glow crimson, pallor puts to flight
The red, no color lingers on her face ;
Her steps are driven to and fro as when
A tiger rages, of its young bereft,                          830
Beside the Ganges in the gloomy woods.
Medea knows not how to curb her love
Or hate.   Now love and hate together rage.
When will she leave the fair Pelasgian fields,
The wicked Colchian one, and free from fear  835
Our king and kingdom ?   Drive with no slow rein
Thy car, Diana ; let the sweet night hide
The sunlight.   Hesperus, end the dreaded day.

# ACT V

## Scene I

*Messenger, Chorus.*

*Messenger* [*enters in haste*].   All are destroyed,
    the royal empire falls,
Father and child lie in one funeral pyre.     840
    *Chorus.*   Destroyed by what deceit?
    *Messenger.*            That which is wont
To ruin princes — gifts.
    *Chorus.*          Could these work harm?
    *Messenger.*   I myself wonder, and can hardly
    deem
The wrong accomplished, though I know it done.
    *Chorus.*   How did it happen?
    *Messenger.*          A destructive fire  845
Spreads everywhere as at command; even now
The city is in fear, the palace burned.
    *Chorus.*   Let water quench the flames.
    *Messenger.*          It will not these,
As by a miracle floods feed the fire.
The more we fight it so much more it glows.  850

## Scene II

*Medea, Nurse.*

*Nurse.*   Up! up! Medea! Swiftly flee the land
Of Pelops; seek in haste a distant shore.

38

*Medea.*  Shall I fly?  I?  Were I already gone
I would return for this, that I might see
These new betrothals.  Dost thou pause, my
      soul?                                          855
This joy's but the beginning of revenge.
Thou dost but love if thou art satisfied
To widow Jason.  Seek new penalties,
Honor is gone and maiden modesty, —
It were a light revenge pure hands could yield.  860
Strengthen thy drooping spirit, stir up wrath,
Drain from thy heart its all of ancient force,
Thy deeds till now call honor; wake, and act,
That they may see how light, how little worth,
All former crime — the prelude of revenge!      865
What was there great my novice hands could dare?
What was the madness of my girlhood days?
I am Medea now, through sorrow strong.
Rejoice, because through thee thy brother died;
Rejoice, because through thee his limbs were
      torn,                                          870
Through thee thy father lost the golden fleece;
Rejoice, that armed by thee his daughters slew
Old Pelias!  Seek revenge!  No novice hand
Thou bring'st to crime; what wilt thou do;
      what dart
Let fly against thy hated enemy?                 875
I know not what my maddened spirit plots,
Nor yet dare I confess it to myself!
In folly I made haste — would that my foe
Had children by this other!  Mine are his,
We'll say Creusa bore them!  'Tis enough;     880

Through them my heart at last finds full revenge;
My soul must be prepared for this last crime.
Ye who were once my children, mine no more,
Ye pay the forfeit for your father's crimes.
Awe strikes my spirit and benumbs my hand;  885
My heart beats wildly; mother-love drives out
Hate of my husband; shall I shed their blood —
My children's blood?   Demented one, rage not,
Be far from thee this crime!   What guilt is theirs?
Is Jason not their father? — guilt enough!        890
And worse, Medea claims them as her sons.
They are not sons of mine, so let them die!
Nay, rather let them perish since they are!
But they are innocent — my brother was!
Fear'st thou?   Do tears already mar thy cheek?  895
Do wrath and love like adverse tides impel
Now here, now there?   As when the winds wage war,
And the wild waves against each other smite,
My heart is beaten; duty drives out fear,
As wrath drives duty.   Anger dies in love.        900
Dear sons, sole solace of a storm-tossed house,
Come hither, he may have you safe if I
May claim you too!   But he has banished me;
Already from my bosom torn away
They go lamenting — perish then to both,        905
To him as me!   My wrath again grows hot;
Furies, I go wherever you may lead.
Would that the children of the haughty child
Of Tantalus were mine, that I had borne
Twice seven sons!   In bearing only two        910
I have been cursed!   And yet it is enough

For father, brother, that I have borne two. —
Where does that horde of furies haste? whom seek?
For whom prepare their fires? or for whom
Intends the infernal band its bloody torch?      915
Whom does Megaera seek with hostile brand?
The mighty dragon lashes its fierce tail —
What shade uncertain brings its scattered limbs?
It is my brother, and he seeks revenge;
I grant it, thrust the torches in my eyes;      920
Kill, burn, the furies have me in their power!
Brother, command the avenging goddesses
To leave me, and the shades to seek their place
In the infernal regions without fear;
Here leave me to myself, and use this hand      925
That held the sword — your soul has found re-
        venge.            [*Kills one of her sons.*
What is the sudden noise?   They come in arms
And think to drive me into banishment.
I will go up on the high roof, come thou;
I'll take the body with me.   Now my soul,      930
Strike! hold not hid thy power, but show the world
What thou art able.
    [*She goes out with the nurse and the living boy,
    and carries with her the body of her dead son.*


## Scene III

*Jason in the foreground, Medea with the children appears
upon the roof.*

*Jason.*   Ye faithful ones, who share
In the misfortunes of your harassed king,

Hasten to take the author of these deeds.          935
Come hither, hither, cohorts of brave men ;
Bring up your weapons ; overthrow the house.
   *Medea.*   I have recaptured now my crown and
      throne,
My brother and my father ; Colchians hold
The golden fleece ; my kingdom is won back ;  940
My lost virginity returns to me !
O gods appeased, marriage, and happy days,
Go now,—my vengeance is complete !  Not yet—
Finish it while thy hands are strong to strike.
Why seek delay ?  Why hesitate, my soul ?     945
Thou art able !  All thine anger falls to nought !
I do repent of that which I have done !
Why did'st thou do it, miserable one ?
Yea, miserable !  Ruth shall follow thee !
'Tis done, great joy fills my unwilling heart,  950
And, lo, the joy increases.  But one thing
Before was lacking — Jason did not see !
All that he has not seen I count as lost.
   *Jason.*   She threatens from the roof ; let fire
      be brought,                                        954
That she may perish burned with her own flame.
   *Medea.*   Pile high the funeral pyre of thy sons,
And rear their tomb.  To Creon and thy wife
I have already paid the honors due.
This son is dead, and this shall soon be so,
And thou shalt see him perish.
   *Jason.*              By the gods,  960
By our sad flight together, and the bond
I have not willingly forsaken, spare

Our son! If there is any crime, 'tis mine;
Put me to death, strike down the guilty one.
   *Medea.*  There where thou askest mercy, and
     canst feel     965
The sting, I thrust the sword.  Go, Jason, seek
Thy virgin bride, desert a mother's bed.
   *Jason.*  Let one suffice for vengeance.
   *Medea.*              Had it been
That one could satisfy my hands with blood,
I had slain none.  But two is not enough.   970
   *Jason.*  Then go, fill up the measure of thy
     crime,
I ask for nothing but that thou should'st make
A speedy end.
   *Medea.*      Now, grief, take slow revenge;
It is my day; haste not, let me enjoy.
                 [*Kills the other child.*
   *Jason.*  Slay me, mine enemy!
   *Medea.*         Dost thou implore   975
My pity?  It is well!  I am avenged.
Grief, there is nothing more that thou canst slay!
Look up, ungrateful Jason, recognize
Thy wife; so I am wont to flee.  The way
Lies open through the skies; two dragons bend
Their necks, submissive to the yoke.  I go   981
In my bright car through heaven.  Take thy sons!
   [*She casts down to him the bodies of her children,*
    *and is borne away in a chariot drawn by dragons.*
   *Jason.*  Go through the skies sublime, and
     going prove     983
That the gods dwell not in the heavens you seek.

# THE DAUGHTERS OF TROY

# THE DAUGHTERS OF TROY

## ACT I

### Scene I

*Hecuba.*  Let him who puts his trust in kingly
    crown,
Who rules in prince's court with power supreme,
Who, credulous of heart, dreads not the gods,
But in his happy lot confides, behold
My fate and Troy's.  Never by clearer proof  5
Was shown how frail a thing is human pride.
Strong Asia's capital, the work of gods,
Is fallen ; and she beneath whose banners fought
The men who drink the Tanais' cold stream
That flows by sevenfold outlet to the sea,  10
And those who see the new-born day where blends
Tigris' warm waters with the blushing strait,
Is fallen ; her walls and towers, to ashes burned,
Lie low amid her ruined palaces.
The flames destroy the city ; far and near  15
Smolders the home of King Assaracus.
But flames stay not the eager conqueror's hand
From plundering Troy.  The sky is hid with
    smoke ;
And day, as though enveloped in black cloud,

47

Is dark with ashes.  Eager for revenge,          20
The victor stands and measures her slow fall;
Forgets the long ten years; deplores her fate;
Nor yet believes that he has vanquished her,
Although he sees her conquered in the dust.
The pillagers are busy with the spoil;          25
A thousand ships will hardly bear it hence.
    Witness, ye adverse deities; and ye,
My country's ashes, and thou, Phrygia's king,
Buried beneath the ruins of thy realm;
Ye spirits of the mighty, in whose life          30
Troy lived; and ye my offspring, lesser shades;—
Whatever ills have happened; whatsoe'er
The priestess of Apollo, to whose word
The god denied belief, has prophesied,
I, going great with child, have earlier feared,          35
Nor feared in silence, though in vain I spoke;—
Cassandra too has prophesied in vain.
Alas, 'twas not the crafty Ithacan,
Nor the companions of his night attack,
Nor Sinon false, who flung into your midst          40
Devouring flame; the glowing torch was mine!
Aged, and sick of life, why weep for Troy?
Unhappy one, recall more recent woes;
The fall of Troy is now an ancient grief!
I've seen the murder of a king — base crime!          45
And, at the altar's foot allowed, I've seen
A baser crime, when Æacus' fierce son,
His left hand in the twisted locks, bent back
That royal head, and drove the iron home
In the deep wound; freely it was received,          50

And buried deep, and yet drawn forth unstained,
So sluggish is the blood of frozen age.
This old man's cruel death at the last mete
Of human life ; and the immortal gods,
Witnesses of the deed ; and fallen Troy's          55
Fair altars, cannot stay the savage hand.
Priam, the father of so many kings,
Has found no grave, and in the flames of Troy
No funeral pyre, and yet the wrathful gods
Are not appeased ; behold, the lot is cast          60
That gives to Priam's daughters and his sons
A master ; and I go to servitude.
This one seeks Hector's wife, this Helenus' ;
And this Antenor's ; nor are wanting those
Who long for thee, Cassandra ; me alone          65
They shun, and I alone affright the Greeks.
    Why cease your lamentations, captive ones ?
Make moan, and smite your breasts, pay funeral
        rites ;
Let fatal Ida, home of your harsh judge,
Reëcho long your sorrowful lament.          70


## SCENE II

*Hecuba, Chorus of Trojan Women.*

*Chorus.*   You bid those weep who are not new
        to grief ;
Our lamentations have not ceased to rise
From that day when the Phrygian stranger sought
Grecian Amyclæ ; and the sacred pine

Of Mother Cybele, through Grecian seas     75
A pathway cut. } Ten times the winter snows
Have whitened Ida — Ida stripped of trees
To furnish Trojan dead with funeral pyres —
Ten times the trembling reaper has gone forth
To cut the bearded grain from Ilium's fields,    80
Since any day has seen us free from tears.
New sorrows ask new mourning, lift thy hand
And beat upon thy breast: thy followers, queen,
Are not inept at weeping.
     *Hecuba.*               Faithful ones,
Companions of my grief, unbind your hair;    85
About your shoulders let it flow defiled
With Troy's hot ashes; come with breast exposed,
Carelessly loosened robes, and naked limbs;
Why veil your modest bosoms, captive ones?
Gird up your flowing tunics, free your hands    90
For fierce and frequent beating of your breasts.
So I am satisfied, I recognize
My Trojan followers; again I hear
Their wonted lamentations. Weep indeed;
We weep for Hector.
     *Chorus.*          We unbind our hair,    95
So often torn in wild laments, and strew
Troy's glowing ashes on our heads; permit
Our loosened robe to drop from shoulders bare;
Our naked bosoms now invite our blows.
O sorrow, show thy power; let Rhœta's
        shores                              100
Give back the blows, nor from her hollow hills
Faint Echo sound the closing words alone,

But let her voice repeat each bitter groan,
And earth and ocean hear.   With cruel blows
Smite, smite, nor be content with faint laments :   105
We weep for Hector.
   *Hecuba.*   For thee our hands have torn our
     naked arms
And bleeding shoulders ;  Hector, 'tis for thee
We beat our brows and lacerate our breasts ;
The wounds inflicted in thy funeral rites   110
Still gape and flow with blood.   Thou, Hector,
     wast
The pillar of thy land, her fates' delay,
The prop of wearied Phrygians, and the wall
Of Troy ;  by thee supported, firm she stood,
Ten years upheld.   With thee thy country fell,   115
Her day of doom and Hector's were the same.
Weep now for Priam, smite for him your breasts ;
Hector has tears enough.
   *Chorus.*   Pilot of Phrygia, twice a captive made,
Receive our tears, receive our wild laments.   120
Whilst thou wast king, Troy suffered many woes ;
Twice by Greek weapons were her walls assailed ;
Twice were they made a target for the darts
Of Hercules ;  and when that kingly band,
Hecuba's offspring, had been offered up,   125
With thee, their sire, the funeral rites were stayed ;
An offering to great Jove, thy headless trunk
Lies on Sigea's plain.
   *Hecuba.*       Women of Troy,
For others shed your tears ;  not Priam's death
I weep ;  say rather all, thrice happy he !   130

Free he descended to the land of shades,
Nor will he ever bear on conquered neck
The Grecian yoke; nor the Atrides see;
Nor look on shrewd Ulysses; nor, a slave,
Carry the trophies on his neck to grace      135
A Grecian triumph; feel his sceptered hands
Bound at his back; nor add a further pomp
To proud Mycene, forced in golden chains
To follow Agamemnon's royal car.
    *Chorus.*   Thrice happy Priam! as a king he
         went                          140
Into the land of spirits; wanders now
Through the safe shadows of Elysian Fields,
In happiness among the peaceful shades,
And seeks for Hector.   Happy Priam say!
Thrice happy he, who, dying in the fight,      145
Bears with him to destruction all his land.

# ACT II

## SCENE I

*Talthybius, Chorus of Trojan Women.*

*Talthybius.* O long delay, that holds the
    Greeks in port,
Whether they seek for war or for their homes.
  *Chorus.* Say what the reason of the long delay,
What god forbids the Greeks the homeward
    road?                    150
  *Talthybius.* I tremble, and my spirit shrinks
    with fear ;
Such prodigies will hardly find belief.
I saw them, I myself; Titan had touched
The mountain summits, dayspring conquered
    night,
When, on a sudden, with a muttered groan,   155
Earth trembled, in the woods the tree-tops shook;
The lofty forests and the sacred grove
Thundered with mighty ruin ; Ida's cliffs
Fell from her summit ; nor did earth alone
Tremble, the ocean also recognized       160
Achilles' coming, and laid bare her depths ;
In the torn earth a gloomy cavern yawned ;
A way was opened up from Erebus
To upper day ; the tomb gave up its dead ;
The towering shade of the Thessalian chief   165

Leaped forth as when, preparing for thy fate,
O Troy, he put to flight the Thracian host,
And struck down Neptune's shining, fair-haired
　　　son;
Or as when, breathing battle from the field,
He filled the rivers with the fallen dead,　　　170
And Xanthus wandered over bloody shoals
Seeking slow channels; or as when he stood
In his proud car, a victor, while he dragged
Hector and Troy behind him in the dust.

　　His wrathful voice rang out along the shore: 175
' Go, go, ye slothful ones, pay honors due
My manes.　Let the thankless ships be freed
To sail my seas.　Not lightly Greece has felt
Achilles' wrath; that wrath shall heavier fall.
Polyxena, betrothed to me in death,　　　180
Must die a sacrifice at Pyrrhus' hand,
And make my tomb glow crimson.'　Thus he
　　　spake,
Shadowed the day with night, and sought again
The realm of Dis.　He took the riven path;
Earth closed above him, and the tranquil sea　185
Lay undisturbed, the raging wind was still,
Softly the ocean murmured, Tritons sang
From the blue deep their hymeneal chant.


## Scene II

*Agamemnon, Pyrrhus.*

*Pyrrhus.*　When, homeward turning, you would
　　fain have spread

Your happy sails, Achilles was forgot.          190
By him alone struck down, Troy fell ; her fall,
Ev'n at his death, was but so long delayed
As she stood doubtful whither she should fall ;
Haste as you will to give him what he asks
You give too late.    Already all the chiefs     195
Have carried off their prizes ; what reward
Of lesser price have you to offer him
For so great valor ?    Does he merit less ?
He, bidden shun the battle and enjoy
A long and happy age, outnumbering          200
The many years of Pylos' aged king,
Threw off his mother's mantle, stood confessed
A man of arms.    When Telephus in vain
Refused Achilles entrance to the coast
Of rocky Mysia, with his royal blood          205
He stained Achilles' hand, but found that hand
Gentle as strong.    When Thebes was overcome
Eëtion, its conquered ruler, saw
His realm made captive.    With like slaughter fell
Little Lyrnessus, built at Ida's foot ;          210
Briseia's land was captured ; Chryse, too,
The cause of royal strife, is overthrown ;
And well-known Tenedos, and Sciro's isle
That, rich with fertile pastures, nourishes
The Thracian herd, and Lesbos that divides     215
The Ægean straits, Cilla to Phœbus dear,
Yes, and whatever land Caïcus laves
With its green depths of waters.    This had been
To any other, glory, honor, fame, —
Achilles is but on the march ; so sped          220

My father, and so great the war he waged
While he made ready for his great campaign.
    Though I were silent of his other deeds,
Would it not be enough that Hector died?
My father conquered Ilium; as for you,            225
You have but made it naught.   It gives me joy
To speak the praises and illustrious deeds
Of my great sire: how Hector in the eyes
Of fatherland and father prostrate fell,
How  Memnon,  too,  lies  slain,  whose  mother
            shuns                                    230
The gloomy light of day, with pallid cheek
Mourning his fate; and at his own great deeds
Achilles trembles, and, a victor, learns
That death may touch the children of a god.
The Amazons' harsh queen, thy final fear,         235
Last yielded.   Wouldst thou honor worthily
His mighty arms, then yield him what he will,
Though he should ask a virgin from the land
Of Argos or Mycene.   Dost thou doubt;
Too soon content, art loth to offer up            240
A maiden, Priam's child, to Peleus' son?
Thy child was sacrificed to Helenus,
'Tis not an unaccustomed gift I ask.
    *Agamemnon.*   To have no power to check the
            passions' glow
Is ever found a fault of youthful hearts;          245
That which in others is the zeal of youth,
In Pyrrhus is his father's fiery heart.
Thus mildly once I stood the savage threats
Of Æacus' fierce son; most patiently

He bears, who is most strong.  With slaughter
  harsh           250
Why sprinkle our illustrious leader's shade?
Learn first how much the conqueror may do,
The conquered suffer.  'Tis the mild endure,
But he who harshly rules, rules not for long.
The higher Fortune doth exalt a man,   255
Increasing human power, so much the more —
Fearing the gods who too much favor him,
And not unmindful of uncertain fate —
He should be meek.  In conquering, I have
  learned
How in a moment greatness is o'erthrown.  260
  Has Trojan triumph too soon made us proud?
We stand, we Greeks, in that place whence Troy
  fell.
Imperious I have been, and borne myself
At times too proudly; Fortune's gifts correct
In me the pride they oft in others rouse.  265
Priam, thou mak'st me proud, but mak'st me fear.
What can I deem my scepter, but a name
Made bright with idle glitter; or my crown,
But empty ornament?  Fate overthrows
Swiftly, nor will it need a thousand ships,  270
Perchance, nor ten years' war.  I own, indeed,
(This can I do, oh Argive land, nor wound
Thy honor) I have troubled Phrygia
And wished her conquered; but I would have
  stayed
The hand that crushed and laid her in the dust. 275
A foe enraged, who gains the victory

By night, checks not his raging at command;
Whatever cruel or unworthy deed
Appeared in any, anger was the cause —
Anger and darkness and the savage sword     280
Made glad with blood and seeking still for more.
    All that yet stands of ruined Troy shall stand,
Enough of punishment — more than enough —
Has been exacted; that a royal maid
Should fall, and, offered as a sacrifice     285
Upon a tomb, should crimson with her blood
The ashes, and this hateful crime be called
A marriage — I will never suffer it.
Upon my head would rest the guilt of all;
He who forbids not crime when he has power,     290
Commands it.
    *Pyrrhus.*         Shall Achilles then go hence
With empty hand?
    *Agamemnon.*         No, all shall tell his praise,
And unknown lands shall sing his glorious name;
And if his shade would take delight in blood
Poured forth upon his ashes, let us slay     295
A Phrygian sheep, rich sacrifice. No blood
Shall flow to cause a sorrowing mother's tears.
What fashion this, by which a living soul
Is sacrificed to one gone down to hell?
Think not to soil thy father's memory     300
With such revenge, commanding us to pay
Due reverence with blood.
    *Pyrrhus.*         Harsh king of kings!
So arrogant while favoring fortune smiles,
So timid when aught threatens! Is thy heart

So soon inflamed with love and new desire;    305
And wilt thou bear away from us the spoil?
I'll give Achilles back, with this right hand,
His victim, and, if thou withholdest her,
I'll give a greater, and whom Pyrrhus gives
Will prove one worthy.  All too long our hand 310
Has ceased from slaughter, Priam seeks his peer.
 *Agamemnon.*   That was, indeed, the worthiest
   warlike act
Of Pyrrhus: with relentless hand he slew
Priam, whose suppliant prayer Achilles heard.
 *Pyrrhus.*   We know our father's foes were
   suppliants,    315
But Priam made his prayer himself, whilst thou,
Not brave to ask, and overcome with fear,
Lurked trembling in thy tent, and sought as aid
The intercessions of the Ithacan
And Ajax.
 *Agamemnon.*   That thy father did not fear, 320
I own; amid the slaughter of the Greeks
And burning of the fleet, forgetting war,
He idly lay, and with his plectrum touched
Lightly his lyre.
 *Pyrrhus.*   Mighty Hector then
Laughed at thy arms but feared Achilles' song; 325
By reason of that fear peace reigned supreme
In the Thessalian fleet.
 *Agamemnon.*   There was in truth
Deep peace for Hector's father in that fleet.
 *Pyrrhus.*   To grant kings life is kingly.
 *Agamemnon.*   Why wouldst thou

With thy right hand cut short a royal life?    330
   *Pyrrhus.*   Mercy gives often death instead of
    life.
   *Agamemnon.*   Mercy seeks now a virgin for
    the tomb?
   *Pyrrhus.*   Thou deemst it crime to sacrifice a
    maid?
   *Agamemnon.*   More than their children, kings
    should love their land.
   *Pyrrhus.*   No law spares captives or denies
    revenge.                                   335
   *Agamemnon.*   What law forbids not, honor's
    self forbids.
   *Pyrrhus.*   To victors is permitted what they
    will.
   *Agamemnon.*   He least should wish to whom is
    granted most.
   *Pyrrhus.*   And this thou sayest to us, who ten
    long years                                 339
Have borne thy heavy yoke, whom my hand
    freed?
   *Agamemnon.*   Is this the boast of Scyros?
   *Pyrrhus.*                         There no stain
Of brother's blood is found.
   *Agamemnon.*                   Shut in by waves —
   *Pyrrhus.*   Nay, but the seas are kin.   I know
    thy house —
Yea, Atreus' and Thyestes' noble house!    344
   *Agamemnon.*   Son of Achilles ere he was a man,
And of the maid he ravished secretly —
   *Pyrrhus.*   Of that Achilles, who, by right of
    race,

Through all the world held sway, inherited
The ocean from his mother, and the shades
From Æacus, from Jupiter the sky.            350
    *Agamemnon.*   Achilles, who by Paris' hand was
        slain.
    *Pyrrhus.*   One whom the gods attacked not
        openly.
    *Agamemnon.*   To curb thy insolence and daring
        words
I well were able, but my sword can spare
The conquered.
        [*To some of the soldiers, who surround him.*
                        Call the god's interpreter.   355
        [*A few of the soldiers go out, Calchas comes in.*


## SCENE III

*Agamemnon, Pyrrhus, Calchas.*

    *Agamemnon.*   [*To Calchas.*]   Thou, who hast
        freed the anchors of the fleet ;
Ended the war's delay ; and by thy arts
Hast opened heaven ; to whom the secret things
Revealed in sacrifice, in shaken earth,
And star that draws through heaven its flaming
        length,                                    360
Are messengers of fate ; whose words have been
To me the words of doom ; speak, Calchas, tell
What thing the god commands, and govern us
By thy wise counsels.
    *Calchas.*               Fate a pathway grants

To Grecians only at the wonted price.              365
A virgin must be slain upon the tomb
Of the Thessalian leader, and adorned
In robes like those Thessalian virgins wear
To grace their bridals, or Ionian maids,
Or damsels of Mycene ; and the bride              370
Shall be by Pyrrhus to his father brought —
So is she rightly wed.   Yet not alone
Is this the cause that holds our ships in port,
But blood must flow for blood, and nobler blood
Than thine, Polyxena.  Whom fate demands— 375
Grandchild of Priam, Hector's only son —
Hurled headlong from Troy's wall shall meet his
        death ;
Then shall our thousand sails make white the
        strait.


## Scene IV

*Chorus of Trojan Women.*

Is it true, or does an idle story
Make the timid dream that after death,              380
When the loved one shuts the wearied eyelids,
When the last day's sun has come and gone,
And the funeral urn has hid the ashes,
He shall still live on among the shades?
Does it not avail to bear the dear one              385
To the grave?   Must misery still endure
Longer life beyond?   Does not all perish
When the fleeting spirit fades in air

Cloudlike?   When the dreaded fire is lighted
'Neath the body, does no part remain?                390
    Whatsoe'er the rising sun or setting
Sees; whatever ebbing tide or flood
Of the ocean with blue waters washes,
Time with Pegasean flight destroys.
Like the sweep of whirling constellations,            395
Like the circling of their king the sun,
Haste the ages.   As obliquely turning
Hecate speeds, so all must seek their fate;
He who touches once the gloomy water
Sacred to the god, exists no more.                    400
    As the sordid smoke from smoldering embers
Swiftly dies, or as a heavy cloud,
That the north wind scatters, ends its being,
So the soul that rules us slips away;
After death is nothing; death is nothing             405
But the last mete of a swift-run race,
Which to eager souls gives hope, to fearful
Sets a limit to their fears.   Believe
Eager time and the abyss engulf us;
Death is fatal to the flesh, nor spares              410
Spirit even; Tænaris, the kingdom
Of the gloomy monarch, and the door
Where sits Cerberus and guards the portal,
Are but empty rumors, senseless names,
Fables vain, that trouble anxious sleep.             415
Ask you whither go we after death?
Where they lie who never have been born.

# ACT III

## Scene I

*Andromache, An Old Man.*

*Andromache.* Why tear your hair, my Phrygian
    followers,
Why beat your breasts and mar your cheeks with
    tears?
The grief is light that has the power to weep. 420
Troy fell for you but now, for me long since
When fierce Achilles urged at speed his car,
And dragged behind his wheel my very self;
The axle, made of wood from Pelion's groves,
Groaned heavily, and under Hector's weight 425
Trembled. O'erwhelmed and crushed, I bore
    unmoved
Whate'er befell, for I was stunned with grief.
I would have followed Hector long ago,
And freed me from the Greeks, but this my son
Held me, subdued my heart, forbade my death, 430
Compelled me still to ask the gods a boon,
Added a longer life to misery.
He took away my sorrow's richest fruit —
To know no fear. All chance of better things
Is snatched away, and worse are yet to come; 435
'Tis wretchedness to fear where hope is lost.

*Old Man.* What sudden fear assails thee, troubled one?

*Andromache.* From great misfortunes, greater ever spring;

Troy needs must fill the measure of her woes.

    *Old Man.* Though he should wish, what can the god do more?     440

    *Andromache.* The entrance of the bottomless abyss

Of gloomy Styx lies open; lest defeat

Should lack enough of fear, the buried foe

Comes forth from Dis. Can Greeks alone return?

Death certainly is equal; Phrygians feel     445

This common fear; a dream of dreadful night

Me only terrified.

    *Old Man.*     What dream is this?

    *Andromache.* The sweet night's second watch was hardly passed,

The Seven Stars were turning from the height;

At length there came an unaccustomed calm     450

To me afflicted; on my eyes there stole

Brief sleep, if that dull lethargy be sleep

That comes to grief-worn souls; when, suddenly,

Before my eyes stood Hector, not as when

He bore against the Greeks avenging fire,     455

Seeking the Argive fleet with Trojan torch;

Nor as he raged with slaughter 'gainst the Greeks,

And bore away Achilles' arms — true spoil,

From him who played Achilles' part, nor was

A true Achilles. Not with flame-bright face     460

He came, but marred with tears, dejected, sad,

Like us, and all unkempt his loosened hair;
Yet I rejoiced to see him.   Then he said,
Shaking his head : ' O faithful wife, awake !
Bear hence thy son and hide him, this alone      465
Is safety.   Weep not !   Do you weep for Troy?
Would all were fallen !   Hasten, seek a place
Of safety for the child.'   Then I awoke,
Cold horror and a trembling broke my sleep.
Fearful, I turned my eyes now here, now there.   470
Me miserable, careless of my son,
I sought for Hector, but the fleeting shade
Slipped from my arms, eluded my embrace.
O child, true son of an illustrious sire ;
Troy's only hope ; last of a stricken race ;       475
Too noble offspring of an ancient house ;
Too like thy father !   Such my Hector's face,
Such was his gait, his manner, so he held
His mighty hands, and so his shoulders broad,
So threatened with  bold  brow  when  shaking
        back                                                480
His heavy hair !   Oh, born too late for Troy,
Too soon for me, will ever come that time,
That happy day, when thou shalt build again
Troy's walls, and  lead  from  flight  her  scattered
        hosts,
Avenging and defending mightily,               485
And give again a name to Troy's fair land ?
But, mindful of my fate, I dare not wish ;
We live, and life is all that slaves can hope.
Alas, what place of safety can I find,
Where hide thee ?   That high citadel, god-built, 490

Is dust, her streets are flame, and naught remains
Of all the mighty city, not so much
As where to hide an infant.   Oh, what place
Of safety can I find?   The mighty tomb,
Reared to my husband — this the foe must fear.
His father, Priam, in his sorrow built,            496
With no ungenerous hand, great Hector's tomb ;
I rightly trust a father.   Yet I fear
The baleful omen of the place of tombs,
And a cold sweat my trembling members bathes. 500
   *Old Man.*   The safe may choose, the wretched
      seize defense.
   *Andromache.*   We may not hide him without
      heavy fear
Lest some one find him.
   *Old Man.*                        Cover up the trace
Of our device.
   *Andromache.*   And if the foe should ask ?
   *Old Man.*   In the destruction of the land he
      died, —                                    505
It oft has saved a man that he was deemed
Already dead.
   *Andromache.*   No other hope is left.
He bears the heavy burden of his name ;
If he must come once more into their power
What profits it to hide him ?
   *Old Man.*                        Victors oft        510
Are savage only in the first attack.
   *Andromache.*   [*To Astyanax.*]   What distant,
      pathless land will keep thee safe,
Or who protect thee, give thee aid in fear ?

O Hector, now as ever guard thine own,
Preserve the secret of thy faithful wife,                    515
And to thy trusted ashes take thy child!
My son, go thou into thy father's tomb.
What, do you turn and shun the dark retreat?
I recognize thy father's strength of soul,
Ashamed of fear.   Put by thy inborn pride,              520
Thy courage; take what fortune has to give.
See what is left of all the Trojan host:
A tomb, a child, a captive!   We succumb
To such misfortunes.   Dare to enter now
Thy buried father's sacred resting-place;                  525
If fate is kind thou hast a safe retreat,
If fate refuse thee aid, thou hast a grave.
       *Old Man.*   The sepulcher will safely hide thy
           son;
Go hence lest thou shouldst draw them to the spot.
       *Andromache.*   One's fear is lightlier borne when
           near at hand,                                         530
But elsewhere will I go, since that seems best.
       *Old Man.*   Stay yet a while, but check the
           signs of grief;
This way the Grecian leader bends his steps.


## Scene II

*Andromache, Ulysses with a retinue of warriors.   [The old man*
                        *withdraws.]*

       *Ulysses.*   Coming a messenger of cruel fate,
I pray you deem not mine the bitter words         535

I speak, for this is but the general voice
Of all the Greeks, too long from home detained
By Hector's child : him do the fates demand.
The Greeks can hope for but a doubtful peace,
Fear will compel them still to look behind      540
Nor lay aside their armor, while thy child,
Andromache, gives strength to fallen Troy.
So prophesies the god's interpreter ;
And had the prophet Calchas held his peace,
Hector had spoken ; Hector and his son      545
I greatly fear : those sprung of noble race
Must needs grow great.   With proudly lifted
      head
And haughty neck, the young and hornless bull
Leads the paternal herd and rules the flock ;
And when the tree is cut, the tender stalk      550
Soon rears itself above the parent trunk,
Shadows the earth, and lifts its boughs to heaven ;
The spark mischance has left from some great fire,
Renews its strength ; like these is Hector's son.
If well you weigh our act, you will forgive,      555
Though grief is harsh of judgment.   We have
      spent
Ten weary winters, ten long harvests spent
In war ; and now, grown old, our soldiers fear,
Even from fallen Troy, some new defeat.
'Tis not a trifling thing that moves the Greeks, 560
But a young Hector ; free them from this fear ;
This cause alone holds back our waiting fleet,
This stops the ships.   Too cruel think me not,
By lot commanded Hector's son to seek ;

I sought Orestes once; with patience bear     565
What we ourselves have borne.
    *Andromache.*                          Alas, my son,
Would that thou wert within thy mother's arms!
Would that I knew what fate encompassed thee,
What region holds thee, torn from my embrace!
Although my breast were pierced with hostile
        spears,                                      570
My hands bound fast with wounding chains, my
        side
By biting flame were girdled, not for this
Would I put off my mother-guardianship!
What spot, what fortune holds thee now, my son?
Art thou a wanderer in an unknown land,     575
Or have the flames of Troy devoured thee?
Or does the conqueror in thy blood rejoice?
Or, snatched by some wild beast, perhaps thou
        liest
On Ida's summit, food for Ida's birds?
    *Ulysses.* No more pretend. Thou mayst not
        so deceive                                   580
Ulysses; I have power to overcome
A mother's wiles, although she be divine.
Put by thy empty plots; where is thy son?
    *Andromache.* Where is my Hector? Where
       the Trojan host?
Where Priam? Thou seek'st one, I seek them
       all.                                          585
    *Ulysses.* What thou refusest willingly to tell,
Thou shalt be forced to say.
    *Andromache.*                          She rests secure

Who can, who ought, nay, who desires to die.
   *Ulysses.*    Near death may put an end to such
     proud boast.
   *Andromache.*    Ulysses, if thou hop'st through
     fear to force                                          590
Andromache to speak, threat longer life;
Death is to me a wished-for messenger.
   *Ulysses.*    With fire, scourge, torment, even
     death itself,
I will compel thy heart's deep-hidden thought;
Necessity is stronger far than death.                      595
   *Andromache.*    Threat flames, wounds, hunger,
     thirst, the bitter stings
Of cruel grief, all torments, sword plunged deep
Within this bosom, or the prison dark —
Whatever angry, fearful victors may;
Learn that a loving mother knows no fear.               600
   *Ulysses.*    And yet this love, in which thou
     standst entrenched
So stubbornly, admonishes the Greeks
To think of their own children.   Even now,
After these long ten years, this weary war,
I should fear less the danger Calchas threats,         605
If for myself I feared — but thou prepar'st
War for Telemachus.
   *Andromache.*              Unwillingly
I give the Grecians joy, but I must give.
Ulysses, anguish must confess its pain;
Rejoice, O son of Atreus, carry back                      610
As thou art wont, to the Pelasgian host
The joyous news: great Hector's son is dead.

*Ulysses.*   How prove it to the Greeks?
*Andromache.*                     Fall on me else
The greatest ill the victor can inflict:
Fate free me by an easy, timely death,                    615
And hide me underneath my native soil!
Lightly on Hector lie his country's earth
As it is true that, hidden from the light,
Deep in the tomb, among the shades he rests.
    *Ulysses.*  Accomplished then the fate of Hector's
        race;                                             620
A joyous message of established peace
I take the Greeks.   [*He turns to go, then hesitates.*
                Ulysses, wouldst thou so?
The Greeks have trusted thee, thou trustest —
        whom?
A mother.   Would a mother tell this lie
Nor fear the augury of dreaded death?                     625
They fear the auguries, who fear naught else.
She swears it with an oath — yet, falsely sworn,
What has she worse to fear?   Now call to aid
All that thou hast of cunning, stratagem,
And guile, the whole Ulysses; truth dies not. 630
Watch well the mother; see — she mourns, she
        weeps,
She groans, turns every way her anxious steps,
Listens with ear attentive; more she fears
Than sorrows; thou hast need of utmost care.
[*To Andromache.*]   For other mothers' loss 'tis
        right to grieve;                                  635
Thee, wretched one, we must congratulate
That thou hast lost a son whose fate had been

To die, hurled headlong from the one high tower
Remaining of the ruined walls of Troy.
 *Andromache* [*aside*].   Life fails, I faint, I fall,
   an icy fear                                    640
Freezes my blood.
 *Ulysses* [*aside*].   She trembles; here the place
For my attack; she is betrayed by fear;
I'll add worse fear.   [*To his followers.*
     Go quickly; somewhere lies,
By mother's guile concealed, the hidden foe —
The Greeks last enemy of Trojan name.          645
Go, seek him, drag him hither.   [*After a pause
  as though the child were found.*]   It is well;
The child is taken; hasten, bring him me.
[*To Andromache.*]   Why do you look around and
   seem to fear?
The boy is dead.
 *Andromache.* Would fear were possible!
Long have I feared, and now too late my soul  650
Unlearns its lesson.
 *Ulysses.*  Since by happier fate
Snatched hence, the lad forestalls the sacrifice,
The lustral offering from the walls of Troy
And may not now obey the seer's command,
Thus saith the prophet: this may be atoned,  655
And Grecian ships at last may find return,
If Hector's tomb be leveled with the ground,
His ashes scattered on the sea; the tomb
Must feel my hand, since Hector's child escapes
His destined death.
 *Andromache* [*aside*].   Alas, what shall I do?  660

A double fear distracts me ; here my son,
And there my husband's sacred sepulcher ,
Which conquers ?   O inexorable gods,
O manes of my husband — my true god,
Bear witness ; in my son 'tis thee I love,          665
My Hector, and my son shall live to bear
His father's image !   Shall the sacred dust
Be cast upon the waves ?   Nay, better death.
Canst thou a mother bear to see him die, —
To   see   him   from   Troy's   tower   downward
          hurled ?                                           670
I can and will, that Hector, after death,
Be not the victor's sport.   The boy may feel
The pain, where death has made the father safe.
Decide, which one shall pay the penalty.
Ungrateful, why in doubt ?  Thy Hector's here! 675
'Tis false, each one is Hector; this one lives,
Perchance th' avenger of his father's death.
I cannot save them both, what shall I do ?
Oh, save the one whom most the Grecians fear !

   *Ulysses.*   I will fulfill the oracle, will raze     680
The tomb to its foundations.

   *Andromache.*                    Which ye sold?

   *Ulysses.*   I'll do it, I will level with the dust
The sepulcher.

   *Andromache.*   I call the faith of heaven,
Achilles' faith, to aid ; come, Pyrrhus, save
Thy father's gift.

   *Ulysses.*               The tomb shall instantly     685
Be leveled with the plain.

   *Andromache.*                    This crime alone

The Greeks had shunned; ye've sacked the holy
    fanes
Even of favoring gods, ye've spared the tomb.
I will not suffer it, unarmed I'll stand
Against your armored host; rage gives me
    strength,        690
And as the savage Amazon opposed
The Grecian army, or the Mænad wild,
Armed with the thyrsus, by the god possessed,
Wounding herself spreads terror through the
    grove,
Herself unpained, I'll rush into your midst,  695
And in defending the dear ashes die.   [*She places
    herself before the grave.*
*Ulysses [angrily to the shrinking soldiers.*
Why pause?   A woman's wrath and feeble noise
Alarms you so?   Do quickly my command.
    [*The soldiers go toward the grave, Androm-*
    *ache throws herself upon them.*
*Andromache.*   The sword must first slay me. —
    Ah, woe is me,
They drive me back.   Hector, come forth the
    tomb;        700
Break through the fate's delay, and overwhelm
The Grecian chief—thy shade would be enough!
The weapon clangs and flashes in his hand;
Greeks, see you Hector?   Or do I alone
Perceive him?
    *Ulysses.*      I will lay it in the dust.  705
    *Andromache [aside].*   What have I done?   To
    ruin I have brought

Father and son together; yet, perchance,
With supplications I may move the Greeks.
The tomb's great weight will presently destroy
Its hidden treasure; O my wretched child,        710
Die wheresoe'er the fates decree, — not here!
Oh, may the father not o'erwhelm the son,
The son fall not upon his father's dust!
           [*She casts herself at the feet of Ulysses.*
Ulysses, at thy feet a suppliant
I fall, and with my right hand clasp thy knees;  715
Never before a suppliant, here I ask
Thy pity on a mother; hear my prayer
With patience; on the fallen, lightly press,
Since thee the gods lift up to greater heights!
The gifts thou grantst the wretched are to fate  720
A hostage; so again thou mayst behold
Thy wife; and old Laertes' years endure
Until once more he see thee; so thy son
Succeed thee and outrun thy fairest hopes
In his good fortune, and his age exceed          725
Laertes', and his gifts outnumber thine.
Have pity on a mother to whose grief
Naught else remains of comfort.
     *Ulysses.*    Bring forth the boy, then thou mayst
          ask for grace.
     *Andromache.*    Come hither from thy hiding-
          place, my son,                          730
Thy wretched mother's lamentable theft.

## SCENE III

*Ulysses, Andromache, Astyanax.*

*Andromache.*   Ulysses, this is he who terrifies
The thousand keels, behold him.   Fall, my son,
A suppliant at the feet of this thy lord,
And do him reverence ; nor think it base,     735
Since Fortune bids the wretched to submit.
Forget thy royal race, the power of one
Renowned through all the world ; Hector forget ;
Act the sad captive on thy bended knee,
And imitate thy mother's tears, if yet     740
Thou feelest not thy woes.   [*To Ulysses.*]   Troy
        saw long since
The weeping of a royal child : the tears
Of youthful Priam turned aside the threats
Of stern Alcides ; he, the warrior fierce
Who tamed wild beasts, who from the shattered
        gates     745
Of shadowy Dis a hidden, upward path
Opened, was conquered by his young foe's tears.
' Take back,' he said, ' the reins of government,
Receive thy father's kingdom, but maintain
Thy scepter with a better faith than he ; '     750
So fared the captives of this conqueror ;
Study the gentle wrath of Hercules !
Or do the arms alone of Hercules
Seem pleasing to thee ?   Of as noble race
As Priam's, at thy feet a suppliant lies,     755
And asks of thee his life ; let fortune give

To whom she will Troy's kingdom.
    *Ulysses.*   Indeed the mother's sorrow moves
      me much!
Our Grecian mothers' sorrow moves me more,
To cause whose bane this child would grow a
      man.                                 760
    *Andromache.*   These ruins of a land to ashes
      burned
Could he arouse? Or could these hands build
      Troy?
Troy has no hope, if such is all remains.
We Trojans can no longer cause thee fear.
And has the child his father's spirit? Yes,   765
But broken. Troy destroyed, his father's self
Had lost that courage which great ills o'ercame.
If vengeance is your wish, what worse revenge
Than to this noble neck to fit the yoke?
Make him a slave. Who ever yet denied   770
This bounty to a king?
    *Ulysses.*             The seer forbids,
'Tis not Ulysses who denies the boon.
    *Andromache.* Artificer of fraud, plotter of guile,
Whose warlike valor never felled a foe;
By the deceit and guile of whose false heart   775
E'en Greeks have fallen, dost thou make pre-
      tense
Of blameless god or prophet? 'Tis the work
Of thine own heart. Thou, who by night mak'st
      war,
Now dar'st at last one deed in open day —
A brave boy's death.

*Ulysses.*                    My valor to the Greeks    780
Is known, and to the Phrygians too well known.
We may not waste the day in idle talk —
Our ships weigh anchor.
  *Andromache.*              Grant a brief delay,
While I, a mother, for my son perform
The last sad office, satiate my grief,              785
My mother's sorrow, with a last embrace.
  *Ulysses.*   I would that I might pity!  What I
      may,
Time and delay, I grant thee; let thy tears
Fall freely; weeping ever softens grief.
  *Andromache.*   O  pledge of love, light of a
      fallen house,                                  790
Last of the Trojan dead, fear of the Greeks,
Thy mother's empty hope, for whom I prayed —
Fool that I was — that thou mightst have the
      years
Of Priam, and thy father's warlike soul,
The gods despise my vows; thou ne'er shalt wield
A scepter in the kingly halls of Troy,              796
Mete justice to thy people, nor shalt send
Thy foes beneath thy yoke, nor put to flight
The Greeks, drag Pyrrhus at thy chariot wheels,
Nor ever in thy slender hands bear arms;           800
Nor wilt thou hunt the dwellers in the wood,
Nor on high festival, in Trojan games,
Lead forth the noble band of Trojan youth;
Nor round the altars with swift-moving steps,
That the reëchoing of the twisted horn             805
Makes swifter, honor with accustomed dance

The Phrygian temples.   Oh, most bitter death !
   *Ulysses.*   Great sorrow knows no limit, cease
      thy moans !
   *Andromache.*   How narrow is the time we seek
      for tears !
Grant me a trivial boon : that with these hands   810
His living eyes be bound.   My little one,
Thou diest, but feared already by thy foes ;
Thy Troy awaits thee ; go, in freedom go,
To meet free Trojans.
   *Astyanax.*        Mother, pity me !
   *Andromache.*   Why hold thy mother's hands
      and clasp her neck,       815
And seek in vain a refuge ?   The young bull,
Thus fearful, seeks his mother when he hears
The roaring of the lion ; from her side
By the fierce lion driv'n, the tender prey
Is seized, and crushed, and dragged apart ; so thee
Thy foeman snatches from thy mother's breast.  821
Child, take my tears, my kisses, my torn locks,
Go to thy father, bear him these few words
Of my complaint : ' If still thy spirit keeps
Its former cares, if died not on the flames    825
Thy former love, why leave Andromache
To serve the Grecians ?   Hector, cruel one,
Dost thou lie cold and vanquished in the grave ?
Achilles came again.'   Take then these locks,
These tears, for these alone I have to give,   830
Since Hector's death, and take thy mother's
      kiss
To give thy father ; leave thy robe for me,

Since it has touched his tomb and his dear dust;
I'll search it well so any ashes lurk
Within its folds.
    *Ulysses.*        Weep no more, bear him hence;
Too long he stays the sailing of the fleet.    835

## Scene IV

*Chorus of Trojan Women.*

What country calls the captives?   Tempe dark?
Or the Thessalian hills? or Phthia's land
Famous for warriors? Trachin's stony plains,
Breeders of cattle? or the great sea's queen,    840
Iolchos? or the spacious land of Crete
Boasting its hundred towns? Gortyna small?
Or sterile Tricca? or Mothone crossed
By swift and frequent rivers?   She who lies
Beneath the shadow of the Œtean woods,    845
Whose hostile bowmen came, not once alone,
Against the walls of Troy?
Or Olenos whose homes lie far apart?
Or Pleuron, hateful to the virgin god?
Or Trœzen on the ocean's curving shore?    850
Or Pelion, mounting heavenward, the realm
Of haughty Prothous?   There in a vast cave
Great Chiron, teacher of the savage child,
Struck with his plectrum from the sounding strings
Wild music, stirred the boy with songs of war.    855
Perchance Carystus, for its marbles famed,
Calls us; or Chalcis, lying on the coast

Of the unquiet sea whose hastening tide
Beats up the strait; Calydna's wave-swept shore;
Or stormy Genoessa; or the isle               860
Of Peparethus near the seaward line
Of Attica; Enispe smitten oft
By Boreas; or Eleusis, reverenced
For Ceres' holy, secret mysteries?
Or shall we seek great Ajax' Salamis?          865
Or Calydon the home of savage beasts?
Or countries that the Titaressus laves
With its slow waters?  Scarphe, Pylos old,
Or Bessus, Pharis, Pisa, Elis famed
For the Olympian games?                        870
It matters not what tempest drives us hence,
Or to what land it bears us, so we shun
Sparta, the curse alike of Greece and Troy;
Nor seek the land of Argos, nor the home
Of cruel Pelops, Neritus hemmed in             875
By narrower limits than Zacynthus small,
Nor threatening cliffs of rocky Ithaca.
O Hecuba, what fate, what land, what lord
Remains for thee? In whose realm meetst thou
        death?

## ACT IV

### Scene I

*Helen, Hecuba, Andromache, Polyxena.*

*Helen* [*soliloquizing*].  Whatever sad and joyless
    marriage bond                    880
Holds slaughter, lamentations, bloody war,
Is worthy Helen.  Even to fallen Troy
I bring misfortune, bidden to declare
The bridal that Achilles' son prepares
For his dead father, and demand the robe    885
And Grecian ornaments.  By me betrayed,
And by my fraud, must Paris' sister die.
So be it, this were happier lot for her ;
A fearless death must be a longed-for death.
Why shrink to do his bidding ?  On the head 890
Of him who plots the crime remains the guilt.
[*Aloud to Polyxena.*
Thou noble daughter of Troy's kingly house,
A milder god on thy misfortune looks,
Prepares for thee a happy marriage day.
Not Priam nor unfallen Troy could give    895
Such bridal, for the brightest ornament
Of the Pelasgian race, the man who holds
The kingdom of the wide Thessalian land,
Would make thee his by lawful marriage bonds.

Great Tethys, and the ocean goddesses,         900
And Thetis, gentle nymph of swelling seas,
Will call thee theirs; when thou art Pyrrhus'
         bride
Peleus will call thee kin, as Nereus will.
Put off thy robe of mourning, deck thyself
In gay attire; unlearn the captive's mien,     905
And suffer skillful hands to smooth thy hair
Now so unkempt.   Perchance fate cast thee down
From thy high place to seat thee higher still;
It may be profit to have been a slave.
         *Andromache.*   This one ill only lacked to fallen
                  Troy:                  910
Pleasure, while Pergamus still smoking lies!
Fit hour for marriage!   Dare one then refuse?
When Helen would persuade, who doubtful weds?
Thou curse!   Two nations owe to thee their fall!
Seest thou the royal tomb, these bones that lie 915
Unburied, scattered over all the field?
Thy bridal is the cause.   All Asia's blood,
All Europe's flows for thee, whilst thou, unstirred,
Canst see two husbands fighting, nor decide
Which one to wish the victor!   Go, prepare   920
The marriage bed; what need of wedding torch
Or nuptial lights, when burning Troy provides
The fires for these new bridals?   Celebrate,
O Trojan women, honor worthily
The marriage feast of Pyrrhus.   Smite your
                  breasts,                  925
And weep aloud.
         *Helen.*               Soft comfort is refused

By deep despair, which loses reason, hates
The very sharers of its grief.   My cause
I yet may plead before this hostile judge,
Since I have suffered heavier ills than she.      930
Andromache mourns Hector openly,
Hecuba weeps for Priam, I, alone,
In secret, weep for Paris.   Is it hard,
Grievous, and hateful to bear servitude?
For ten long years I bore the captive's yoke.   935
Is Ilium laid low, her household gods
Cast down?   To lose one's land is hard indeed —
To fear is worse.   Your sorrow friendship cheers,
Me conquerors and conquered hate alike.
For thee, there long was doubt whom thou
        shouldst serve,                            940
My master drags me hence without the chance
Of lot.   Was I the bringer of the war?
Of so great Teucrian carnage?   Think this true
If first a Spartan keel thy waters cut;
But if of Phrygian oars I am the prey,          945
By the victorious goddess as a prize
Given for Paris' judgment, pardon me!
An angry judge awaits me, and my cause
Is left to Menelaus.   Weep no more,
Andromache, put by thy grief.   Alas,           950
Hardly can I myself restrain my tears.
    *Andromache.*   How great the ill that even
        Helen weeps!
Why does she weep?   What trickery or crime
Plots now the Ithacan?   From Ida's top,
Or Troy's high tower, will he cast the maid      955

Upon the rocks? Or hurl her to the deep
From the great cliff which, from its riven side,
Out of the shallow bay, Sigeon lifts?
What wouldst thou cover with deceitful face?
No ill were heavier than this: to see                960
Pyrrhus the son of Priam's Hecuba.
Speak, plainly tell the penalty thou bringst.
Take from defeat at least this evil,—fraud.
Thou seest thou dost not find us loth to die.
    *Helen.*  Would that Apollo's prophet bade me
        take                965
The long delay of my so hated life;
Or that, upon Achilles' sepulcher,
I might be slain by Pyrrhus' cruel hand,
The sharer of thy fate, Polyxena,
Whom harsh Achilles bids them give to him —
To offer to his manes, as his bride                971
In the Elysian Fields.
    [*Polyxena shows great joy, Hecuba sinks faint-
        ing to the ground.*
    *Andromache.*  See with what joy a noble woman
        meets
Death-sentence, bids them bring the royal robe,
And fitly deck her hair.  She deemed it death 975
To be the bride of Pyrrhus, but this death
A bridal seems.  The wretched mother faints,
Her sinking spirit fails; unhappy one,
Arise, lift up thy heart, be strong of soul!
Life hangs but by a thread — how slight a thing 980
Glads Hecuba!  She breathes, she lives again,
Death flies the wretched.

*Hecuba.*                    Lives Achilles still
To vex the Trojans?   Still pursues his foes?
Light was the hand of Paris ; but the tomb
And ashes of Achilles drink our blood.          985
Once I was circled by a happy throng
Of children, by their kisses weary made,
Parted my mother love amongst them all.
She, now, alone is left; for her I pray,
Companion, solace, healer of my grief,          990
The only child of Hecuba, her voice
Alone may call me mother!   Bitter life,
Pass from me, slip away, spare this last blow!
Tears overflow my cheeks — a storm of tears
Falls from her eyes!
   *Andromache.*          We are the ones should
      weep,                                     995
We, Hecuba, whom, scattered here and there,
The Grecian ships shall carry far away.
The maid will find at least a sepulcher
In the dear soil of her loved native land.
   *Helen.*  Thy own lot known, yet more thou'lt
      envy hers.                                1000
   *Andromache.*  Is any portion of my lot un-
      known?
   *Helen.*  The fatal urn has given thee a lord.
   *Andromache.*  Whom call I master?   Speak,
      who bears me hence
A slave?
   *Helen.*  Lot gave thee to the Scyrian king.
   *Andromache.*  Happy Cassandra, whom Apollo's
      wrath                                     1005

Spared from such fate!
   *Helen.*      The prince of kings claims her.
   *Hecuba.*   Be glad, rejoice, my child; Androm-
       ache
Desires thy bridals, and Cassandra, too,
Desires them.   Is there any one would choose
Hecuba for his bride?
   *Helen.*           Thou fallst a prey   1010
To the unwilling Ithacan.
   *Hecuba.*          Alas,
What powerless, cruel, unrelenting god
Gives kings by lot to be the prey of kings?
What god unfriendly thus divides the spoil?
What cruel arbiter forbids us choose   1015
Our masters?  With Achilles' arms confounds
Great Hector's mother?
               To Ulysses' lot!
Conquered and captive am I now indeed,
Besieged by all misfortunes!  'Tis my lord
Puts me to shame, and not my servitude!   1020
Harsh land and sterile, by rough seas enclosed,
Thou wilt not hold my grave!  Lead on, lead on,
Ulysses, I delay not, I will go—
Will follow thee; my fate will follow me.
No tranquil calm will rest upon the sea;   1025
Wind, war, and flame shall rage upon the deep,
My woes and Priam's!  When these things shall
      come,
Respite from punishment shall come to Troy.
Mine is the lot, from thee I snatch the prize!
But see where Pyrrhus comes with hasty steps 1030

And troubled face.  Why pause?  On, Pyrrhus,
       on!
Into this troubled bosom drive the sword,
And join to thy Achilles his new kin!
Slayer of aged men, up, here is blood,          1034
Blood worthy of thy sword; drag off thy spoil,
And with thy hideous slaughter stain the gods —
The gods who sit in heaven and those in hell!
What can I pray for thee?  I pray for seas
Worthy these rites; I pray the thousand ships,
The fleet of the Pelasgians, may meet          1040
Such fate as that I fain would whelm the ship
That bears me hence a captive.


## Scene II

   *Chorus.*  Sweet is a nation's grief to one who
       grieves —
Sweet are the lamentations of a land!          1044
The sting of tears and grief is less when shared
By many; sorrow, cruel in its pain,
Is glad to see its lot by many shared,
To know that not alone it suffers loss.
None shuns the hapless fate that many bear;
None deems himself forlorn, though truly so,  1050
If none are happy near him.  Take away
His riches from the wealthy, take away
The hundred cattle that enrich his soil,
The poor will lift again his lowered head;
'Tis only by comparison man's poor.          1055

O'erwhelmed in hopeless ruin, it is sweet
To see none happy.   He deplores his fate
Who, shipwrecked, naked, finds the longed-for
      port
Alone.   He bears with calmer mien his fate   1059
Who sees, with his, a thousand vessels wrecked
By the fierce tempest, sees the broken planks
Heaped on the shore, the while the northwest
      wind
Drives on the coast, nor he alone returns
A shipwrecked beggar.   When the radiant ram,
The gold-fleeced leader of the flock, bore forth
Phryxus and Helle, Phryxus mourned the fall   1066
Of Helle dropped into the Hellespont.
Pyrrha, Deucalion's wife, restrained her tears,
As he did, when they saw the sea, naught else,
And they alone of living men remained.        1070
The Grecian fleet shall scatter far and wide
Our grief and lamentations.   When shall sound
The trumpet, bidding spread the sails?   When
      dip
The laboring oars, and Troy's shores seem to flee?
When shall the land grow faint and far, the sea
Expand before, Mount Ida fade behind?        1076
Then grows our sorrow; then what way Troy lies
Mother and son shall gaze.   The son shall say,
Pointing the while, 'There where the curving
      line
Of smoke floats, there is Ilium.'   By that sign
May Trojans know their country.        1081

# ACT V

## Scene I

*Hecuba, Andromache, Messenger.*

*Messenger.*   O bitter, cruel, lamentable fate!
In these ten years of crime what deed so hard,
So sad, has Mars encountered?   What decree
Of fate shall I lament?   Thy bitter lot,          1085
Andromache?   Or thine, thou aged one?
　　*Hecuba.*   Whatever woe thou mournst is
　　　　Hecuba s;
Their own griefs only others have to bear,
I bear the woes of all, all die through me,
And sorrow follows all who call me friend.          1090
　　*Andromache.*   Suffering ever loves to tell its
　　　　woes,
Tell of the deaths — the tale of double crime;
Speak, tell us all.
　　*Messenger.*　　　　One mighty tower remains
Of Troy, no more is left; from this high seat
Priam, the arbiter of war, was wont          1095
To view his troops; and in this tower he sat
And, in caressing arms, embraced the son
Of Hector, when that hero put to flight
With fire and sword the trembling, conquered
　　　　Greeks.
From thence he showed the child its father's deeds.

This tower, the former glory of our walls,    1101
Is now a lonely, ruined mass of rock;
Thither the throng of chiefs and people flock;
From the deserted ships the Grecian host
Come pouring; on the hills some find a place, 1105
Some on the rising cliffs, upon whose top
They stand tiptoe; some climb the pines, and
     birch,
And laurel, till beneath the gathered crowd
The whole wood trembles; some have found the
     peaks
Of broken crags; some climb a swaying roof, 1110
Or toppling turret of the falling wall;
And some, rude lookers-on, mount Hector's
     tomb.
Through all the crowded space, with haughty
     mien,
Passes the Ithacan, and by the hand
Leads Priam's grandson; nor with tardy step 1115
Does the young hero mount the lofty wall.
Standing upon the top, with fearless heart
He turns his eagle glance from side to side.
As the young, tender cub of some wild beast,
Not able yet to raven with its teeth,      1120
Bites harmlessly, and proudly feels himself
A lion; so this brave and fearless child,
Holding the right hand of his enemy,
Moves host and leaders and Ulysses' self.
He only does not weep for whom all weep,    1125
But while the Ithacan begins the words
Of the prophetic message and the prayers

To the stern gods, he leaps into the midst
Of his and Priam's kingdom, willingly.
   *Andromache.*   Was ever such a deed by Col-
       chians done,                                                    1130
Or wandering Scythians, or the lawless race
That dwells beside the Caspian?   Never yet
Has children's blood Busiris' altars stained,
Nor Diomedes feasted his fierce steeds
On children's limbs!   Who took thy body up,
My son, and bore it to the sepulcher?      1136
   *Messenger.*   What would that headlong leap
       have left?   His bones
Lie dashed in pieces by the heavy fall,
His face and noble form, inheritance
From his illustrious father, are with earth      1140
Commingled; broken is his neck; his head
Is dashed in pieces on the cruel stones
So that the brains gush forth; his body lies
Devoid of form.
   *Andromache.*      Like Hector, too, in this.
   *Messenger.*   When from the wall the boy was
       headlong cast                                                 1145
And the Achaians wept the crime they did,
Then turned these same Achaians to new crimes,
And to Achilles' tomb.   With quiet flow
The Rhœtean waters beat the further side,
And opposite the tomb the level plain      1150
Slopes gently upward, and surrounds the place
Like a wide amphitheater; here the strand
Is thronged with lookers-on, who think to end
With this last death their vessels' long delay,

And glad themselves to think the foeman's seed
At last cut off.   The fickle, common crowd    1156
Look coldly on ; the most part hate the crime.
The Trojans haste with no less eagerness
To their own funeral rites, and, pale with fear,
Behold the final fall of ruined Troy.              1160
As at a marriage, suddenly they bring
The bridal torches ; Helen goes before,
Attendant to the bride, with sad head bent.
' So may the daughter of Hermione
Be wed,' the Phrygians pray, ' base Helen find
Again her husband.'   Terror seizes both       1166
The awe-struck peoples.   With her glance cast
          down,
Modestly comes the victim ; but her cheeks
Glow, and her beauty shines unwontedly ;
So shines the light of Phœbus gloriously       1170
Before his setting, when the stars return
And day is darkened by approaching night.
The throng is silenced ; all men praise the maid
Who now must die : some praise her lovely form,
Her tender age moves some, and some lament
The fickleness of fortune ; every one            1176
Is touched at heart by her courageous soul,
Her scorn of death.   She comes, by Pyrrhus
          led ;
All wonder, tremble, pity ; when the hill
Is reached, and on his father's grave advanced,
The young king stands, the noble maid shrinks
          not,                                                  1181
But waits unflinchingly the fatal blow.

Her unquelled spirit moves the hearts of all;
And — a new prodigy — Pyrrhus is slow
At slaughter; but at length, with steady hand,
He buries to the hilt the gleaming sword    1186
Within her breast; the life-blood gushes forth
From the deep wound; in death as heretofore
Her soul is strong; with angry thud she falls
As she would make the earth a heavy load    1190
Upon Achilles' breast.   Both armies weep;
The Trojans offer only feeble moans;
The victors mourn more freely.   So was made
The sacrifice; her blood lay not for long
Upon the soil, nor flowed away; the tomb    1195
Drank cruelly the gore.
    *Hecuba.*              Go, conquering Greeks,
Securely seek your homes; with all sail set,
Your fleet may safely skim the longed-for sea.
The lad and maid are dead, the war is done!
Where can I hide my woe, where lay aside    1200
The long delay of the slow-passing years?
Whom shall I weep? my husband, grandson,
      child,
Or country?   Mourn the living or the dead?
O longed-for death, with violence dost thou
      come
To babes and maidens, but thou fleest from me!
Through long night sought, mid fire, and swords,
      and spears,    1206
Why fly me?   Not the foe, nor ruined home,
Nor flame could slay me, though so near I stood
To Priam!

*Messenger.*    [*Talthybius, coming from the Greek camp.*

Captive women, seek with speed
The sea ; the sails are filled, the vessels move.    1210

www.ingramcontent.com/pod-product-compliance
Ingram Content Group UK Ltd.
Pitfield, Milton Keynes, MK11 3LW, UK
UKHW041417200125
4192UKWH00035B/382